TURNING BOWLS:
STEP-BY-STEP

TURNING BOWLS:
STEP-BY-STEP

David Regester

B.T. BATSFORD LTD · LONDON

To Christine

First published 1994

Typeset by Best-set Typesetter Ltd., Hong Kong

Printed and bound in Great Britain by
BPC Hazell Books Ltd
A member of
The British Printing Company Ltd

Published by
B.T. Batsford Ltd
4 Fitzhardinge Street
London W1H 0AH

A CIP catalogue record for this book is available
from the British Library

ISBN   0 7134 7239 1

CONTENTS

INTRODUCTION

A bowl is a vessel for holding things, and since it is hollow it has to be mounted on the lathe so that its middle can be removed. In this book I describe the techniques to enable you to do this and explore how to make some of the many different types of bowl that are possible. I also discuss design principles in an attempt to enable you to develop your own style from a sound basis.

I do not pretend to be an expert on all the possible ways of turning bowls; who could when there are as many different ways of turning as there are turners? What I do offer are detailed descriptions of the methods I use that I have developed while turning full-time since 1974. I learnt these methods largely from trial and error but have picked up vital tips from some good friends and books along the way. Personal tuition from a good teacher will augment what I have to say and I suggest that you keep an open mind and try methods that work for other people. I have found that even if other people's ideas do not work for me they have often sparked off ideas of my own. It makes no sense to condemn a method of work on any basis except that it is unsafe or does not work for you.

PART ONE

EQUIPMENT, MATERIALS AND DESIGN

EQUIPMENT

In this book I do not describe in any detail how to equip the workshop as this is covered in *Woodturning: Step-by-Step*, but I do list the basic equipment you need with particular reference to bowl turning.

LATHE

If you have already made up your mind that bowls are going to be your main interest then you will almost certainly want to make large bowls eventually. If this is the case then you should try to buy a lathe that has a swing of about 225 mm (9 in), has a motor of at least $\frac{3}{4}$ hp, and preferably $1\frac{1}{2}$ hp, and is solidly built so that it will be stable when it has a large blank mounted on it.

Some lathes are made so that the swing between centres is relatively small and they cater for the turning of large bowls by having an outboard rest arm with a greater swing. This is a better system than the one where the motor swings around because there are no fixings to adjust (or to work loose) and the rest support is quite solid, the main disadvantage being that the work rotates in the opposite direction on this side which can cause problems

to some people. In addition, you can only use the chucks on one side or the other unless you get an adaptor or have them specially engineered to enable them to fit both sides. Tools such as the half round scraper will only be useable on one side of the lathe. That said, these are minor problems compared to working over the lathe bed.

You will need a range of speeds to cater for different sizes of blanks and the slowest of these should be 450 rpm or less. If you can afford a lathe which has the facility for varying the speed with the turn of a switch rather than moving a belt onto different pulleys, then you will find this even more of a boon in bowl turning than spindle turning. This is because you tend to need to change the speed more often when turning bowls than spindles either to cater for different sizes of blanks or to counter the wobbling induced by a blank having different densities within it. A bowl may well vibrate at one speed but not at a slightly faster or slower one.

The height of the lathe is important because you should not need to bend over when using it as this puts a great strain on the back. The usual advice is to set the lathe so that the elbow is level with the

centre of the spindle but I have found that it is better if the lathe is some 50 mm (2 in) higher than this. It is always healthier to have to reach up than to bend down.

Chucks

Where you need to hollow one end of a piece of work, as in the case of bowls, you need to support the other end by means of a chuck. There is a wide variety of chucks available now and it is very difficult to decide which one to buy, but see Chapter 4 for a thorough examination of some of the best.

BENCH GRINDER

The other essential piece of equipment is a bench grinder for sharpening your tools. There is no greater bar to good turning than blunt tools and there is no better way of sharpening them than with an ordinary bench grinder fitted with soft white aluminium oxide grindstones. These are specifically made for high speed tools but sharpen carbon steel just as well. I recommend that you have one 60 grit for the first rough grind and one 100 grit for a honing grind, but if you only want one grindstone, an 80 grit stone gives a pretty good edge. When using a 100 grit stone it is most important not to press too hard as the tool will very rapidly overheat and lose its temper.

CHAINSAW

A chainsaw is a dangerous piece of equipment, but then so is a car. The difference is that you cannot use the latter on a highway without passing your test whereas anyone can go into a shop and buy a chainsaw and use it on their own premises for their own benefit without a minute's training. The legal position in Great Britain is covered by the Health and Safety at Work Act 1974 which does not specifically refer to chainsaws, but there are moves towards greater regulation and the only way to be sure of the up-to-date legal position is to ask the appropriate Government Department. You may well find that you can do what you like on your own land but as soon as you start to use one for profit on anyone else's land you may need to go on a course and obtain a certificate. If you are thinking of buying or hiring a chainsaw it makes sense to take a course even if you only intend to use it on your own land. It just might save a very unpleasant injury.

If you have the skill and training you can prepare your bowl blanks using only a chainsaw but it makes life a bit easier if you also have a bandsaw, which will enable you to cut blanks more accurately. If you are not going to turn any bowls larger than 450 mm (18 in) in diameter, then a two wheel saw with 250 mm (10 in) between blade and body is big enough. It is the depth of cut that is most critical for the bowl turner and if you can obtain a bandsaw with the capacity to cut 250 mm (10 in) deep you should be able to cater for most eventualities.

BASIC TOOLS AND SHARPENING

The basic tools needed for turning bowls (**fig. 1**) comprise two 12.5 mm ($\frac{1}{2}$ in) deep fluted bowl gouges; one 6.25 mm ($\frac{1}{4}$ in) deep fluted bowl gouge; one 37.5 mm (1$\frac{1}{2}$ in) wide, 9.37 mm ($\frac{3}{8}$ in) section half round scraper; one 12.5 mm ($\frac{1}{2}$) in, 6.25 mm ($\frac{1}{4}$ in) section square ended scraper and a 9.37 mm ($\frac{3}{8}$ in) drill bit set in a tool handle for establishing the depth of the bowl. In addition to this you will need a rule, pencil, pair of dividers, hammer, screwdriver, bradawl, vegetable oil and beeswax. I sometimes use other tools for specific purposes and mention these as and when required.

There are two main types of steel used in turning tools, carbon steel and high speed steel. Carbon steel is perfectly adequate, indeed all turners used to use it, but high speed steel is better because it holds its edge so much longer. This makes

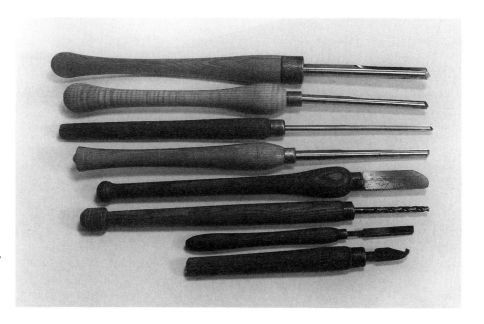

Fig. I
Basic tool kit

it better value even though it initially costs more.

I make my own handles for tools because I have the wood anyway and I can make each one different so that I can recognize which tool is which when the business ends are lost in a pile of shavings. You may notice that my tool handles are shorter than some people like to have them. That is because I do not think that long handles are necessary. You ought to turn so that all the work is done by the lathe motor not your arms. All you need to do is present the tool at the correct angle.

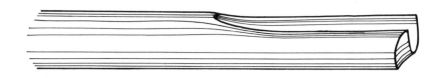

Fig. 2
Deep fluted bowl gouge, straight across
12.5 mm ($\frac{1}{2}$ in)

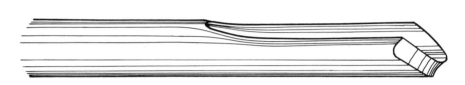

Fig. 3
Deep fluted bowl gouge, ground back
12.5 mm ($\frac{1}{2}$ in)

Deep fluted bowl gouge 12.5 mm ($\frac{1}{2}$ in)

Fig. 4 shows a close up of the gouges I use. The flute of a gouge is the channel that runs most of its length. Gouges made for bowl turning often have deep flutes, for two reasons: first, because the tools are made of thick stock to absorb the heat generated by the hard work the tools have to do and second, so that the tools do not break or flex too much when projecting over the tool rest.

I like to have at least two of these gouges available for use at any one time; one with the edge ground square (**fig. 2**), more or less as supplied, and the other with the edge ground back (**fig. 3**), which is useful for getting inside tight curves inside a bowl (**fig. 5, page 14**) and has a long side edge which can be used for fine finishing cuts (see **fig. 91, page 69**).

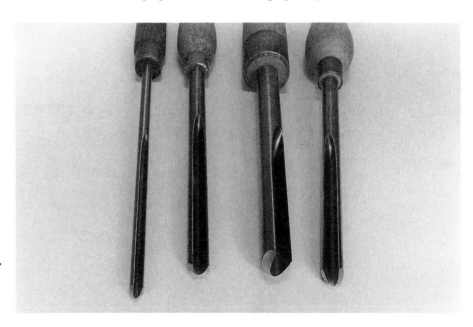

Fig. 4
Close up of gouges

This tool is one of the more difficult ones to sharpen and in **figs. 6a–c** below, you can see that the tool has to be swung across the wheel so that at the start the tool is right over on the left side and at the end it is right over on the right, the mirror image of **a** in the sequence. You should always sharpen so that the scratches left by the stone are at right angles to the edge of the tool, and grinding should start at the bevel and work towards the edge so that only at the very end of the sharpening process are the sparks going over the edge into the flute of the gouge. You can tell when a tool is sharp if there is no light reflected from the edge.

Fig. 5
Ground back gouge inside bowl

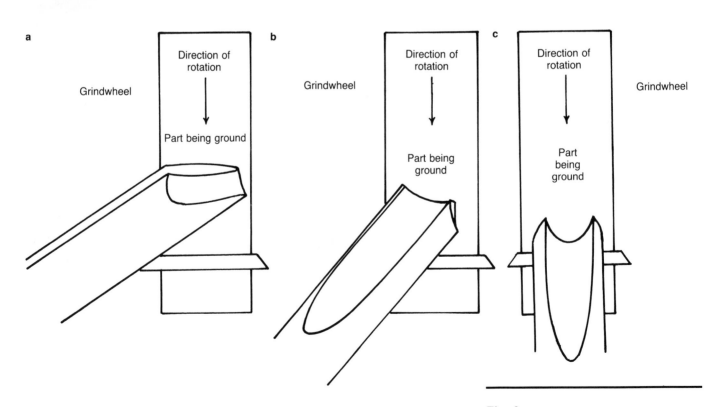

Fig. 6a–c
Grinding ground back gouge

Deep fluted bowl gouge 18.75 mm ($\frac{3}{4}$ in)

This tool is useful for big bowls because the greater bulk absorbs any vibrations and it takes off bigger shavings.

Deep fluted bowl gouge 6.25 mm ($\frac{1}{4}$ in)

I like to have one of these with a ground back edge for the finest finishing cuts (**fig. 125**, **page 88**); being of thinner section it is easier to get a fine edge on this than on the thicker tools.

Square ended scraper 12.5 mm ($\frac{1}{2}$ in) (**fig. 7**)

The square ended scraper I use is not exactly square but ground at a few degrees off the square to form a dovetail when pressed straight into the work parallel with the axis. I grind the left hand side of the tool so that the top edge slightly overhangs the bottom edge to prevent the bottom edge fouling the side of the dovetail.

It is a standard tool but I sharpen it with a longer bevel than usual because I find that this cuts better. I like to cut with an edge rather than with the burr that is thrown up by the grinder as this does not last very long when pressed against a piece of wood that is rotating fast.

Half round scraper 37.5 mm ($1\frac{1}{2}$ in)

This is another standard tool but I grind the bevel a lot longer than standard so that it can be used pointing upwards for the smoothing cut inside bowls (**fig. 8**). This gives a better finish off the tool than the normal way with the edge below the level of the rest, but it is a difficult cut for the novice and something to be only tried when you have sufficient confidence to handle the tool very lightly.

Fig. 7
Close up of scrapers

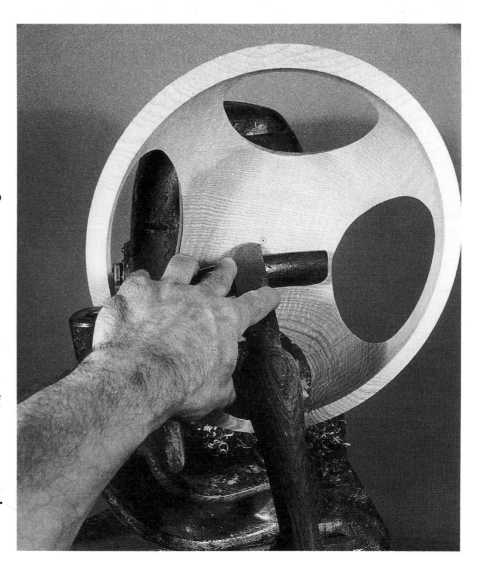

Fig. 8
Scraper inside bowl, pointing up

TOOL USE – GENERAL RULES

The only inviolable rule is to keep your tools sharp. Blunt tools do not cut cleanly and encourage you to use more and more force to get the tool to cut which can only end in disaster. In *Woodturning: Step by Step* I describe in some detail how to sharpen tools but the most important thing to remember is: if you think your tool might be blunt – sharpen it!

Most tools cut best in most applications with the bevel rubbing on the wood or very close. So, if you are trying out a new tool or find that you are having trouble using a tool, go back to basics and rub the bevel on the work, gradually moving the tool so that the edge starts to produce fine shavings, and then pushing the tool along or into the wood at that angle. Also, when trying a new tool or new technique, hold the tool against the wood before starting the lathe so that you can see at what angles you can hold the tool such that the bevel rubs, and then rotate the wood by hand to see if it produces shavings. Start with the lathe at a slow speed until you are confident and then a faster speed when you are ready. There are no hard and fast rules about lathe speed but if the blank is regular and is not heavier on one side due to differences in density or water content, I would turn 100 mm (4 in) deep bowls of the following diameters at these speeds if my lathe just had stepped pulleys and not variable speeds: 150 mm (6 in) to 200 mm (8 in) at 1330 rpm, 225 mm (9 in) to 325 mm (13 in) at

Fig. 9
Using gouge on inboard side of lathe, right-handed

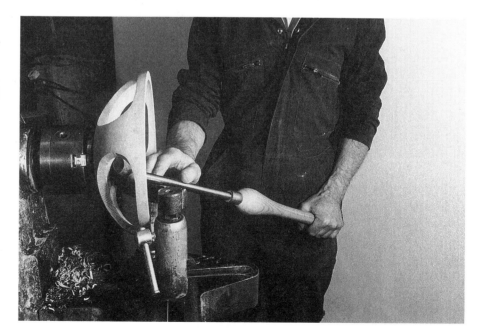

Fig. 10
Using gouge on inboard side of lathe, left-handed

790 rpm and 350 mm (14 in) to 450 mm (18 in) at 425 rpm. With variable speeds available I start at slower speeds than these and increase the speed depending on whether the blank is rotating evenly and how the wood is responding to the gouge.

There is no reason why you should use your stronger hand on the rest or the end of the handle since both hands work just as hard. There will be occasions when it is easier to approach the work using one hand rather than the other so it is best to practise using both hands at the rest. In **fig. 9** I am holding a gouge on the inboard side of the lathe in the usual right-handed manner and in **fig. 10** I am holding the gouge in the usual left-handed manner. **Figs. 11–12** show right- and left-handed poses for the outboard side.

If you are trying a new technique it makes a lot of sense to practise on a piece of cheap unseasoned wood so that you get the technique right before using a piece of expensive wood that you might waste. After all, you would not expect to write a book without first learning to write each individual letter.

Fig. 11
Using gouge on outboard side of lathe, right-handed

Fig. 12
Using gouge on outboard side of lathe, left-handed

ABRASIVES

Garnet paper is the cheapest type of abrasive I would recommend, but the grits do tend to detach from the paper when it is damp or where it is folded. Once the grits get into the wood there is no way you can use the tools again without blunting them. If you do use garnet paper, however, I recommend that you use the lightest papers because they are the most flexible when sanding around curves.

The best abrasives are coated, cloth-backed aluminium oxide where the grits do not have the same tendency to become loose. This type of abrasive also cuts more efficiently than garnet and leaves a smoother finish. Though initially more expensive than garnet, since it lasts a lot longer it works out cheaper in the end.

A useful selection of grits to have is 80, 100, 180 and 240. When you have got as good a finish from the tool as possible you start with the lowest number and only when you have removed all the areas of rough grain do you progress to the next grade. You then eradicate the marks left by the coarse grade with ever finer grades. If you keep the abrasive moving all the time you should avoid making very deep grooves, and if you fold the abrasive in three you will protect your fingers from getting too hot. It is better to hold the abrasive so that if it catches on the work it will be pulled out of your hand not pushed into it (see **fig. 13**).

Abrasives can alter the shape of what you have turned but you should only do this consciously. To avoid accidentally blurring your nice fine detailing you should cut the abrasive into small strips and only sand one face at a time. Too much sanding not only spoils the sharpness of some detail but can also change the cross-section from circular to oval which can be a big fault in certain cases. This effect is called differential sanding and is caused by some parts of the wood being more easily eroded than others.

Fig. 13
Sanding with hand held abrasive

SAFETY FIRST

The workshop is a potentially dangerous place because of the presence of electricity, sharp-edged tools and machines capable of rotating large lumps of wood at high speeds. The best way to handle these dangers is to keep your workshop tidy and well organized. Most safety rules are common sense, but that sense can be put to the back of the mind by tiredness or when the creative urge is driving you.

There are two periods in their career when the turner is particularly prone to self inflicted damage: the first is when unfamiliarity with tools and processes leads to mistakes and the second is when familiarity has bred contempt. After you have had a nasty and painful experience with a tool you tend to associate it with pain and thereafter be careful. The time of day when you are most likely to have an accident is in the afternoon when most of us feel tired for an hour or two. If your attention is wandering and you find yourself thinking of something other than what you are doing, it is time to have a break.

Perhaps the worst hazard is the least obvious and that is dust. It is easy to ignore this until you find that your lungs or sinuses have suffered irrevocable damage. In Britain and the States you have a statutory duty to control this hazard and it is in your best interest to use an efficient personal air filter and a dust extractor. The lathe itself is potentially dangerous because the wood can detach itself and become an unguided missile. To minimize this risk:

- Double check that the wood is firmly held on the lathe.

- Where possible avoiding standing to the side of work held at only one end such as on a faceplate as this is the direction in which it is most likely to fly.

- Always turn the wood by hand before starting the lathe to see that nothing will snag it.

- Check the speed before you turn it on (it is a good idea to leave the lathe set at a slow speed so that if you forget to check there should be no danger).

- Keep a line of retreat open so that you can run away from a potential disaster while you think what to do about it.

- Always wear some sort of eye protection.

2

WOOD

The next thing you will need is some wood. As a result of the growing popularity of turning you can now buy blanks already prepared for turning from several leading timber merchants as well as some of the smaller saw mills. This was not the case when I started turning in 1974 but for the beginner this is an excellent way to get started because it enables you to make your first bowl without having to invest in any sophisticated cutting equipment. It also means that you can try out a wide range of different woods without buying great quantities of each. The down side of this is that, in order to cover the time involved in preparation and the wastage factors unavoidable when converting timber, these blanks work out much more expensive than the price you would have to pay at the timber yard for wood in the plank.

The cheapest, and most environmentally friendly source of supply, is to obtain your own locally-grown timber perhaps when it has been blown down in a storm or when a garden tree has outlived its usefulness. If offered a tree that is still standing it is vital to make sure it can be legally felled as in some countries such as New Zealand you

may need to get a permit, and in England you may find that the tree is in a conservation area. If you spread the word around that you can use such timber you should get some interesting offers. Many trees that are grown for their ornamental and fruit bearing characteristics are also very good for turning and even if they prove to be less decorative or easy to turn than you would like they will usually only cost the time and trouble that you take to fetch them. You will probably find that a bowl given in exchange for the tree will ensure that the word is passed on to the neighbours that here is a way of getting rid of what to them may well be a worthless encumbrance. All you will need to tap into this free supply is a means of transport and a chainsaw.

CUBIC CAPACITY

When you are offered a tree it may be that you will need to assess the volume of the wood either because you will be asked to pay for it at a certain rate per cubic metre or cubic foot or because you need to be able to work out the weight so that you will know whether you will be able

to carry it on the form of transport you have.

If trees were square in cross-section there would be no problem but they are more or less round. The way the trade assesses the cubic capacity of a tree with the bark still on involves the use of a system of measurement which is too complicated to go into here but is designed to take into account standard amounts for loss in conversion which varies with the use to which the tree is to be put. If you just want a rough idea of the cubic capacity for the purpose above, use the following method.

Measure the length and then estimate its average radius. If you assume it is a true cylinder and work out the volume using the area of the circle (π[3.1415] × radius squared) multiplied by the length, you will have a rough idea of the volume. A more accurate way is to measure the girth at about halfway along and divide this by four (known as the quarter girth). If you assume what experience has taught others, i.e. that this figure is what the four sides of the tree would measure if it were square, you get the volume of the tree by multiplying the width of one side by itself and then by the length.

You can use the volume to work out the sort of price you should offer for timber in the round if you can find out what the current figure is in your locality, and you can use it to work out the likely weight by consulting one of the reference books on timber for the average weight per cubic unit. The weight given in such books is for dry timber so you will need to double this figure for a rough idea of the weight of timber in the round, for the wood is sure to be fairly wet. There is a useful list of the commoner timbers in *The Woodworker's Pocket Book* by Charles H Haywood (published by Harper Collins), and they vary from chestnut at 35lb per cubic foot and oak at 45lb to 52lb to boxwood at 54lb to 70lb dry weight.

TIMBER CONVERSION

I shall cover this topic in more detail in the subsequent chapters, but the basic principle stems from the way the wood lays down its cells, in other words its organic structure. The function of timber is to support the leaves of the tree and to carry water and minerals up to them so that photosynthesis can take place. Trees have evolved the most efficient way of doing this which is to lay down their cells in the form of tubes which run from top to bottom.

The above facts have the following consequences:

- A recently felled tree contains a lot of liquid, particularly if it is felled during the growing season.

- Timber has more lengthways than lateral strength.

- You get a different response from cutting the timber in one direction rather than another.

- Wood is more porous through the end grain than across the grain.

The first point above means that after the tree has been felled it will lose water to the atmosphere until its water content is in equilibrium with the relative humidity of the air. During this process the timber shrinks, but because of the structure, this effect occurs more across the grain than along it. It also takes place more rapidly at the exposed ends than in the middle and certain types of cell formation within a given piece of wood change volume at a different rate to others. The drying process therefore sets up tensions that are resolved by splitting and warping. You have to bear all this mind when you prepare a piece of tree for turning.

How you prepare the wood depends on how you intend to use it, but if you get a log and want to keep your options open you should first split it down its length, either with a chainsaw or wedges, to prevent it developing radial shakes. Then seal the ends either with 'End grain sealer' (emulsified paraffin wax), PVA glue or any old paint you have lying around. This slows down the rate of transpiration from the ends (which also causes cracking). Store the wood out of the sun and rain, but accessible to any playful zephyr to aid drying.

You will get a lot of wastage if you cut logs into short lengths because water transpires very quickly from the ends and this results in cracking because the middle does not dry as rapidly as the ends. Short slices often crack all the way through and are only of use on the fire.

The other three bullet points (stated in the second column) mean that it is unusual for bowls to be made with the grain running from top to the bottom: first, because if the bowl has a thin bottom it will have a tendency for the bottom to crack if much pressure is placed upon it; second, because a bowl that is used for salad will have a tendency to leak salad dressing through the short end grain; and third, that it is easier to gouge out the middle of a bowl cutting with the grain if it is aligned at right angles to the lathe axis.

This last point is one of the most important to bear in mind when deciding how you are going to cut any piece of wood. Wood always cuts easier and cleaner if you do it so that the fibres you are cutting are supported by the fibres underneath. For example, you always sharpen a pencil with a knife cutting from the outside to the lead – never in the other direction.

COSTING WORK

One very pleasant aspect of the growth in woodturning is that many professionals are prepared to pass on their knowledge to any individual or group who make it worth their while. This willingness to share can be encouraged if the knowledge is put to use in producing high quality pieces of work so that the general public's opinion of turning is raised. Unfortunately that opinion is not enhanced if the items are sold at cheap prices, for low price is often associated with low quality.

If you do make some good pieces that you are willing to sell, it is to the benefit of all in the long run if you price them using the same criteria as a professional would. This involves taking into account not only the price of the wood and other materials but also a reasonable rate for the time taken and the inclusion of the cost of heating, renting and insuring the workshop. If you also remember that a professional also has to earn enough to pay for the bookwork, design time, selling and putting enough by to pay for a pension you will have some idea of how efficient he has to be to make his work at a price that will sell.

3
DESIGN

The word design means different things to different people but I will only use it to refer to the fact that every object, whether made by man or nature, can be drawn and described in such detail that, given the manufacturing techniques, it could be reproduced. In other words the design of an object is a working drawing.

The *process* of designing, however, does not require that a working drawing is produced. Whenever you make anything the design process is involved even though it may be entirely unconscious. If you make a sand castle you do not think 'I must first produce a design taking into account the purpose of the castle, the materials available and my skill as a sand castle builder', but that is what you do. It is only when the design process is described in words that it gets complicated and that is simply because we do not normally talk about it, so we are not familiar with the words to describe it.

I want to talk about design in connection with turning wooden bowls because, unlike making sandcastles, the purpose of the exercise is to produce a permanent object which may or may not have a practical function but certainly ought to look good. It is too easy to

practise techniques and not think about whether the object produced has any merit over and above being a cleverly shaped piece of wood. You can get away with this in woodturning because the material is often so beautiful that the attention of the observer is distracted from any deficiencies there may be in the design.

Very often all you can say about a piece of indifferent turning is that it is a beautiful piece of wood. Well, this should not please the turner because the wood was there before he ever got hold of it. If the next comment is that it is well finished, then some credit may be taken, but the ultimate compliment is that it is a good design.

Good design does not often happen by accident, and it is only by studying the subject that you can learn to design things that are consistently beautiful and functional. The easiest way to design a bowl is to copy someone else's work, but you only really know if that bowl is well designed if you have learned to appreciate what makes a good design. You may well say that the person who made the bowl is a well known turner and therefore the bowl must be well designed, but a moment's thought

should reveal the many flaws in that line of reasoning.

DESIGN BASICS

If you really want to learn how to design then you should go back to basics. Unfortunately there are no mathematical formulae that you can apply to any given object to establish its design status. There are, however, some questions you can ask which will help you to reach an opinion:

● Does it perform its function?

● Do you like the shape?

The answer to the first question is obvious in the case of a utilitarian object such as a salad bowl, but if it does not seem to be particularly suited to any purpose you can only assume that its function is decorative or perhaps that it carries some message about the human condition. What the turner intended is not relevant, and you should base your opinion on what you see and how you respond to it for it is perfectly possible that a bowl that was intended as a salad bowl might strike you as being so beautiful that any consideration of practical purpose is transcended, just as a bowl that may have been intended to carry some deep message may strike you as being ideal to hold your prized collection of beer mats.

As for the second question, this is the nitty gritty and is entirely subjective. There are certainly some shapes that have a more universal appeal than others but I would be very surprised if there was a shape that appealed to no one.

Why do some shapes have more universal appeal?

The fact that there are some shapes that appeal to more people than others implies to me that there is some in-built mechanism at work. Very many of the plants and animals that share our world are considered beautiful and I think that is because they have conditioned our ideas of what constitutes beauty.

Not only are natural things very likely candidates for the objects that have formed our inherited ideas of beauty but also there can be no doubt that in a design sense a flower that has been successfully passing on its genes for millions of years fulfils its function and therefore satisfies that aspect of good design. If you really want to learn about design I would suggest that studying nature is the best route. If you are interested in the academic arguments about the relationship between design and nature, however, there are several books listed in the back which I can

recommend as great thought provokers.

How to learn to design

Studying nature is the most rigorous way of learning good design but the next best way is to study anything man-made for they have all been designed. You may choose to decide for yourself which of these items accord with your ideas of good design or you may choose to concentrate your study on the objects that are generally thought of as being well designed i.e. those objects that have won awards or have stood the test of time. Good sources for these are museums and art galleries.

I must point out that the purpose of this study is to develop your own ideas on design, not to copy the designs of others. You may think that the shape of a particular bowl in ceramics or glass is so lovely that you must reproduce it in wood but beware, for a certain shape can succeed in one medium but it does not necessarily translate to another. That said, there is no harm in trying it to see if it does.

The following are some ideas about design that I think are useful. I hope that they will help but you should reach your own conclusions.

AESTHETICS

A well made bowl is a very satisfactory object because it has an outer and inner space. The lines of

its external shape, viewed from a distance, can be simply graceful or rugged, or elaborately ornamental, and the internal shape can echo the external or contrast with it. It can feel smooth or rough, light or heavy. It can satisfy, mystify or repel and when made of wood it can show you more of the structure of wood than any other object made of wood since it has an outer and an inner surface.

All hand made bowls in wood or clay are, by definition, works of art but I have yet to see the bowl that is by common consensus a 'Great Work of Art' in the same way that a sculpture or painting may be. This is because to achieve this lofty status it is generally thought that a work of art should say something to the observer rather than simply being what it is, however beautiful it may be.

The more closely the form of the bowl is allied to its function the further it may be said to be from a 'Great Work of Art'. This is perhaps because for it to be recognized as a salad bowl, for instance, it needs to be similar to other salad bowls and it is difficult to see beyond this for any 'message'.

Whether this is a fault in the bowl or the observer is a moot point but it means that the attempt to push the genre into 'Art' status by some turners has resulted in the form of the bowl being pushed beyond any functional application and indeed losing the label 'bowl' in favour of 'hollow form'. These explorations of the genre have involved wet turning, enclosed forms and decoration with paint; all of which can be attractive if done well.

Form and function

Two common functions of bowls are to hold salad or fruit. A good salad bowl requires a depth of 100 mm (4 in) to 150 mm (6 in) and sides curving slightly inwards so that the salad can be tossed with sufficient vigour and not have the contents splashed around the table (see Chapter 5 and figs. **14**–**15**). A fruit bowl should not be as deep because the fruit should not be piled so high that it gets squashed, and it can have a more open shape so that it displays its contents (**fig. 16**). It is even better if it has a few holes in it to allow the air to circulate! Individual bowls for side salads, soup or breakfast cereals are commonly 150 mm (6 in) wide and 75 mm (3 in) to 100 mm (4 in) deep.

The size of the base should flow from the shape of the sides and should be sufficiently wide to make the bowl stable without making it so wide that it looks clumsy. It is not possible to be any more precise. If there were any inviolable mathematical relationship it would be a very boring world. However, as you can see from **fig. 15**, if you follow the outside shape with your

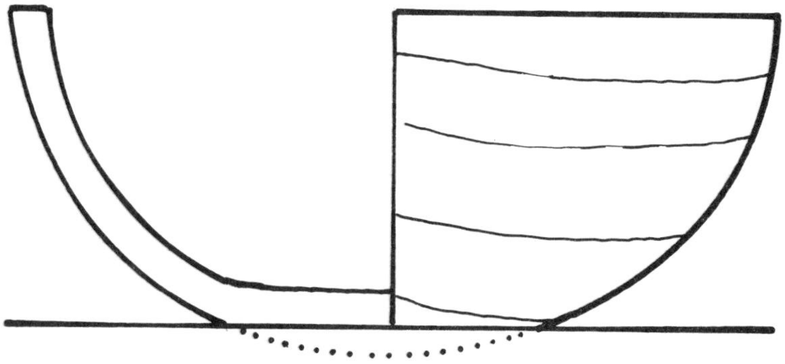

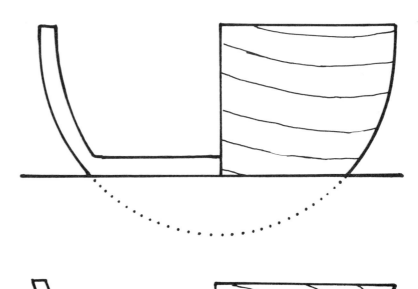

Fig. 14
Light design for salad bowl

Fig. 15
Heavy design for salad bowl

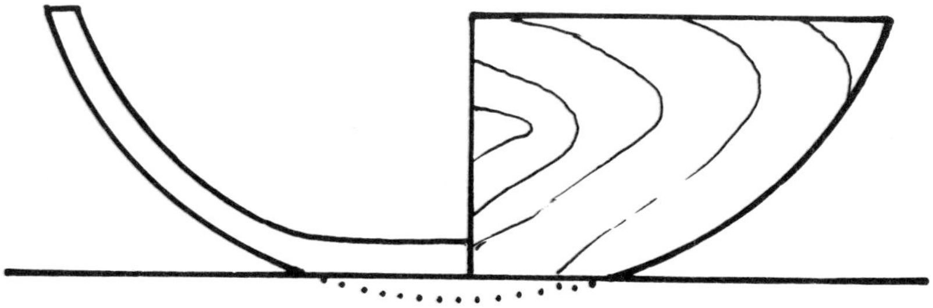

Fig. 16
Light design for fruit bowl

eye and the line disappears deep below the surface it is standing on, it will look heavy and, as you can see from **figs. 14, 16 and 17**, if the line goes just under the surface it will look light. If the base has a rounded bottom it will look very light but be rather unstable!

A foot of the right size such as in **figs. 18–21** will also have the effect of 'lightening' the bowl. Beware of making the foot too tall, however, because everyone will know that the only reason for wasting the wood by not making the bowl as deep inside as possible is that there

was some fault in the wood. It is very hard to shape a tall base so that it looks totally convincing.

With regard to thickness it is often said that the walls should be of even thickness and you can always tell a connoisseur by the way they run their hands down the inside and

Fig. 17
Light burr elm bowl

Fig. 18
Footed ash bowl

outside of a bowl at once to see if this is so. The reason why this rule holds good is that an even wall thickness results in a bowl that is as heavy as it looks. If it has a thin lip and a thick bottom, it will be heavier than you think it ought to be. On the other hand, a rim that overhangs the inside so that the walls get thinner as they go down casts a shadow on the inside of the bowl that enhances the volume of the bowl and makes the inside more mysterious and look deeper (**figs. 22–23**).

It is up to you to use this knowledge to confirm or confront the observer's expectations.

Bowls intended for a practical purpose should be thick enough to stand frequent use. Hopefully the person who owns it will use it and wash it so that it develops a patina and this process inevitably involves

Fig. 19
Footed laburnum bowls

Fig. 20
Footed burr oak bowl

Fig. 21
Footed burr ash bowl

Fig. 22
Overhung lip of ash bowl

Fig. 23
Overhung lip of yew bowl

the occasional bowl/floor interaction that can shatter too flimsy a design. Fruit bowls can look good with wide rims particularly when the wood has got a beautiful grain, because the grain might not be visible inside the bowl if it is full of fruit.

The design of the rim gives some scope for personal expression but on a salad bowl there should not be too much detail because it will be harder to clean. Likewise, if the grain is particularly beautiful, I prefer to avoid any ornamentation that might detract from the appreciation of this. As with any other design decisions the most effective rims are the definite ones (**fig. 24**). If you decide to make the rim flat, then the edges should be quite crisp but not so sharp that they are not finger friendly. The flat rim does not need to be dead square but I have found that an inward slope is more successful than an outward one, which I think is to do with the way an inwards slope would tend to make anything placed on the edge go into the bowl, which is what it is for. An outward slope tends to reject potential contents and lead the eye away from the bowl.

Proportion

I have already alluded to the inadvisability of relying on a mathematical formula to determine the relationship of base to bowl. I have never designed anything in accordance with the 'Golden section' of Euclid or the Fibonacci series but I have analysed some bowl proportions in these terms and it is interesting to note how the proportions of diameter to depth and base size to depth of some particularly satisfying bowl shapes conform fairly closely to the length/breadth ratio of 1 : 0.618 which is the Golden mean (**figs. 25–27, page 30**).

Of course most bowls are made to the maximum depth of the wood available rather than according to the ideal proportions. There are not many turners who would make a bowl shallower than it could be because it would waste wood which costs money, and I cannot argue with this.

If you examine the figures, you will see that if you analyse the proportions of the common size of individual salad bowl 150 mm (6 in) wide 100 mm (4 in) deep by dividing the depth by the diameter you get the figure of 0.666 which is close to the Golden section. It is also interesting to note that if you draw profiles of bowls with bases the same size as these in the figures, then construct rectangles on these bases to the height of the bowls as in the figures, you will find that each rectangle has proportions that fairly closely approach the Golden section. If you enlarge the size of the bowl, say to 250 mm (10 in) by 150 mm (6 in) and to 375 mm (15 in) by 225 mm (9 in), as in the diagrams, it is self evident that the width/depth ratio remains close to the Golden section.

I do not suggest for one minute that you always follow these ratios, because it is much better to develop your eye so that you can make your shapes to please yourself. I would

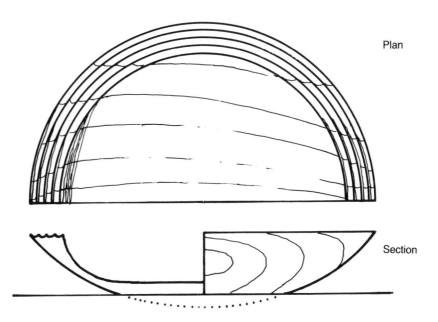

Plan

Section

Fig. 24
Design for shallow bowl with grooved lip

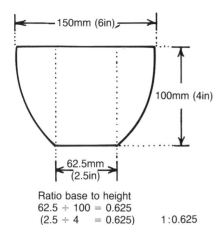

Ratio height to width
100 ÷ 150 = 0.666
(4 ÷ 6 = 0.666)
1 : 0.666

Golden mean = 1 : 0.618

150mm (6in)

100mm (4in)

62.5mm
(2.5in)

Ratio base to height
62.5 ÷ 100 = 0.625
(2.5 ÷ 4   = 0.625)   1 : 0.625

Fig. 25

Relating dimensions of 150 mm (6 in) ×
100 mm (4 in) bowl to Golden mean

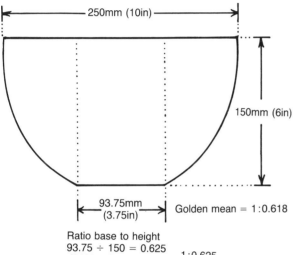

250mm (10in)

150mm (6in)

Ratio height to width
150 ÷ 250 = 0.6
(6 ÷ 10 = 0.6)
1 : 0.6

93.75mm
(3.75in)   Golden mean = 1 : 0.618

Ratio base to height
93.75 ÷ 150 = 0.625
(3.75 ÷ 6   = 0.625)   1 : 0.625

Fig. 26

Relating dimensions of 250 mm (10 in) ×
150 mm (6 in) bowl to Golden mean

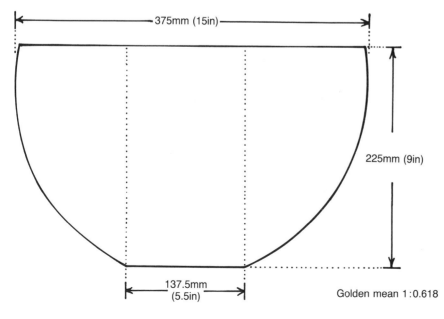

375mm (15in)

225mm (9in)

Ratio height to width
225 ÷ 375 = 0.6
(9 ÷ 15   = 0.6)
1 : 0.6

137.5mm
(5.5in)

Golden mean 1 : 0.618

Ratio base to height 137.5 ÷ 225 = 0.61   1 : 0.61
(5.5 ÷ 9   = 0.61)

Fig. 27

Relating dimensions of 375 mm (15 in) ×
225 mm (9 in) bowl to Golden mean

suggest, however, that if you find a particular bowl pleasing and wish to discover why, you may find that part of the answer lies in how closely the proportions relate to the Golden section.

I almost invariably make my bowls with continuously curved sides because that is the type of shape I feel happiest with, probably because I want my bowls to be handled and that is the shape of two cupped hands. But if you wish to make a bowl with sides that incorporate changes of direction and perhaps ridges and grooves (and do not trust your own judgement), check it out with Euclid but also bear in mind the following points:

- If you are going to have a change of direction in a curve then make it definite for if you do not you will not convince the observer that it is 'meant to be'.

- If you are going to incorporate grooves or ridges into the design it is more satisfying to make one, two, three or five. These are the first four figures in the Fibonacci series which are generated by adding each number to the previous one, and, incidentally, if you divide the first term by the second and the second by the third and so on the quotient tends to 0.618034, our old friend the Golden section.

I have incorporated ridges in the side of the bowl in **fig. 28** (see chapter 5, pages 72 and 73, for how this was done) and because they are low down on the side of the bowl they are generally in shadow and

therefore not immediately visible. You only really notice them when you pick up the bowl and this is an unexpected and not unpleasant surprise if you are expecting a smooth sensation. I would like to be able to say that this was what I intended when I made the grooves but must confess that it is a happy accident.

Shape

Inspiration for the shape of bowls can be sought all around you if you have the eyes to see. The curve is the most natural shape, for nature eschews the straight line. Look at the curves of hills, branches of trees, petals and the silhouettes of animals and humans. But do not just look. Make yourself draw them even if you do not consider yourself to be a

good draughtsman: it is surprising what you can teach yourself to do if you try hard enough.

I would like to reiterate the warning, however, that not all shapes that you see will work in wood from both practical and aesthetic points of view. Wood is a warm, living material with its own intrinsic surface detail and a dimension that few other materials have, namely smell. Ceramics have no smell, and are cold to the touch, but because of their lack of intrinsic interest are a wonderful opportunity for the potter to express himself in a wide variety of shapes and decoration. If you decide to emulate any design feature that a potter has used please ask yourself before you start why you are incorporating this into a wooden

Fig. 28
Ribbed side of ash bowl, upside down

bowl. Does it add to what you are doing?

Keeping the above reservations in mind there is a book called *Ceramic Form* by Peter Lane (see Recommended Reading) that contains several pages of profiles many of which would translate to the medium of wood most satisfactorily. To see if they work, try out a succession of profiles on a piece of cheap wood, removing it from the lathe to view it from a normal angle after finishing each profile.

FINISH

There are four questions to bear in mind when applying finish to a bowl:

- Is it compatible with the use to which it will be put?

- Does it enhance the aesthetic impression you wish to give?

- Has it harmed the environment to produce it?

- Will it harm you to apply it?

If a bowl is intended to be used for food then the finish should not have a strong smell nor be poisonous, and it should respond favourably to being washed.

The finish that I use to satisfy these criteria is cooking oil and beeswax. I apply a small amount of oil when the work is stationary (**fig. 29**) and the wax is held against the work as it rotates (**fig. 30**). One pass of the wax over the surface is

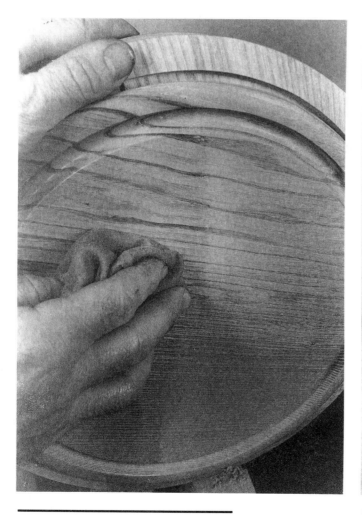

Fig. 29
Applying vegetable oil

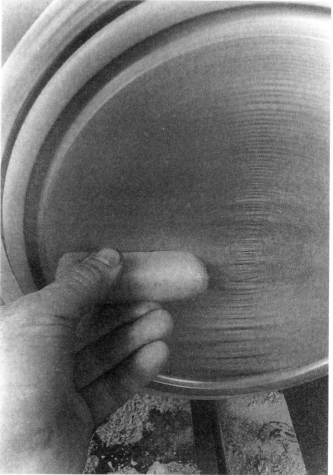

Fig. 30
Applying beeswax

sufficient and it is then buffed with a cloth. The oil makes the wood look good and inhibits the absorption of food flavours. If the user wishes to renew the finish it is commonly found in kitchens.

When repeatedly washed this finish gradually becomes less visible but the wood acquires a patina that is much better than any finish you can deliberately apply. **Figs. 31 and 32** are of a 150 mm (6 in) × 100 mm

(4 in) individual salad bowl which has been in use for about 12 years and all that has been done to it is regular washing and the incidental application of whatever substances have come from the food eaten

Fig. 31
Patina on outside of 12-year-old ash side salad bowl

Fig. 32
Patina inside same bowl

from it. It has not been the source of any food poisoning incidents! **Fig. 33** is of an equally old, elm breadboard that has been scored by countless passes of the bread knife and looks all the better for it.

There has been a movement led by kitchen suppliers and Government agencies in the USA and Europe against the use of wood in kitchens, particularly for chopping boards, in favour of non-porous materials which are supposed to offer bacteria (such as Salmonella) less chance of surviving to contaminate other food. New research by Dean O. Oliver and Nese O. Ak (two Microbiologists at the University of Wisconsin-Madison) as reported in *Science News* (Volume 143, 6 February 1993), has indicated to the contrary, for they found that within three minutes of inoculating wooden boards with cultures of common food poisoning agents 99.9 per cent were unrecoverable and presumed dead.

When the researchers maintained plastic boards overnight at high humidity and room temperature, the microbe population grew – in contrast to wood where no live bacteria were recovered the following morning. But if the wood had been treated with mineral oil to make it more impermeable the

Fig. 33
12-year-old elm breadboard

bacteria survived longer. Whether vegetable oil would have the same effect I doubt because it is more readily biodegradable.

Certainly, from an aesthetic point of view, oil suits me because it is not shiny. High gloss finishes reflect light from the surface which interferes with the visibility of the grain patterns of the wood. These finishes also tend to have a hard, cold feel which to me is not compatible with the warm, variable textures of wood.

If you do want a shiny finish, perhaps because the wood does not have a very interesting grain, then I suggest that you avoid the sort of finish that forms a film over the surface, such as varnish. Apart from the fact that this interferes with the feel of the wood, you will also find that as the wood moves and parts of the bowl are subject to wear, the finish will need renovating which involves removing the old finish. This is not an easy job.

On some ornamental pieces I use Danish oil or Tung oil. These are absorbed into the wood and although you can build up quite a shiny surface you can also leave them matt. They do have some problems in so far as they may contain chemical drying agents which smell and may be toxic (perhaps only until they have dried).

They are also highly inflammable which means that they must be used with care and any rags used to apply them must be disposed of carefully allowing for their tendency to spontaneously combust.

PART TWO

TECHNIQUES

-4-

CHUCKING

The main difference between spindle and faceplate turning is that whereas a spindle is usually supported at both ends so that the outside can be turned, bowls and flatware such as breadboards are usually held on the lathe on some sort of chuck, so that the faces are free to be turned. There are three stages in making a bowl:

- **Fig. 34** shows five ways of mounting for turning the bottom before hollowing.

- **Fig. 35** (page 40) shows five ways of mounting for hollowing.

- **Fig. 36** (page 40) shows five ways of mounting for turning the bottom after hollowing.

These are only some of the methods you can use but they are ones that I have found to be particularly useful. At the end of each method I describe how to remove the chuck if it gets stuck.

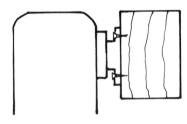

a Single-screw chuck

b Faceplate

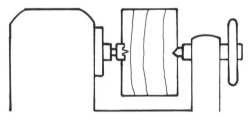

c Between centres

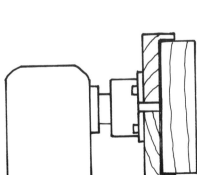

d Axminster four-jaw chuck with wood plates

e Four-jaw chuck with external jaws

Fig. 34a–e
Five ways to mount a bowl blank for turning bottom

39

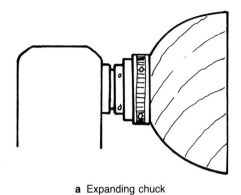

a Expanding chuck

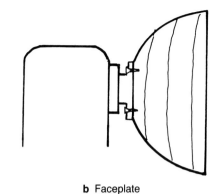

b Faceplate

Fig. 35a–e
Five ways to mount a bowl blank for hollowing

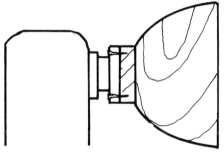

c Faceplate holding block glued to base of bowl

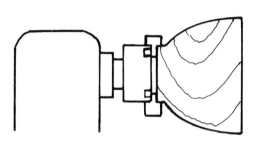

d Four-jaw chuck with external jaws

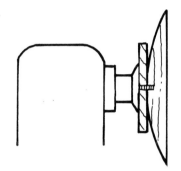

e Single-screw chuck

Fig. 36a–e
Five ways to mount a bowl blank for turning the bottom after hollowing

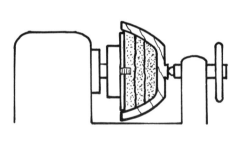

a Between centres using foam discs

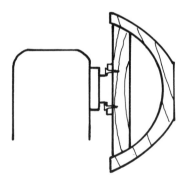

b Wooden chuck held on faceplate (tailstock support optional)

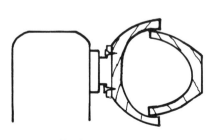

c Bowl held on faceplate as jam chuck

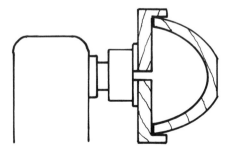

d Axminster four-jaw with wood plates

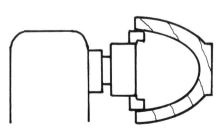

e Four-jaw chuck with external jaws expanded inside bowl

FACEPLATE

When starting with a blank that has true faces, i.e. that has been cut from a plank that was competently sawn, you can use a faceplate through which screws pass into the blank (**fig. 37**). This is fine for turning the base of a bowl when the screw holes will be removed by the subsequent hollowing process, but the bowl needs to be remounted after the base has been turned flat and if this is done with screws, the holes will be left in the base. I used to do all my bowls like this and I filled the holes with plastic wood – they sold very well! **Fig. 38** shows the bottom of the salad bowl in **figs. 31–32**, on page 33, and you can see that the plastic wood has survived remarkably intact. I then discovered that glue (firstly epoxy resin and then cyanoacrylate) mixed with wood dust constituted a stronger and even better camouflaged alternative.

There are several disadvantages to this method: one is that the filled holes are still visible and bother some people, another is that I prefer to keep the use of chemicals in the workshop to an absolute minimum because I am not sure how safe they are and what the environmental cost of their production is. The length of the screws will also dictate the depth of the base of the bowl. Furthermore, accurately re-centring a bowl on a faceplate is not easy and the act of screwing in the screws both time consuming and hard on the wrists. As you get more expert, decrease the length of the screws or use a plywood washer between the faceplate and bowl.

Fig. 37
Faceplate on bottom of bowl blank

Fig. 38
Bottom of 12-year-old side salad bowl
showing holes filled with plastic wood

Removal of faceplates

If you keep the threads of the shaft and the faceplate clean and well oiled, do not have too many big catches and do not leave the faceplate on the lathe too long (it is particularly important not to let a warm faceplate and shaft cool in contact), then faceplates should not get stuck too often. If one does get stuck, do the following.

Hold the shaft of the lathe still by whatever means appropriate (such as a spanner) and, as hard as possible, rotate the blank held on the faceplate in the unwinding direction. If this does not shift it try jerking it abruptly in the correct direction. This often works if the piece is relatively large but if you persist with the method too long you can tear the screws out of the wood. If jerking fails you will need to remove the work from the faceplate which requires a cranked screw driver. You can perhaps buy one that incorporates a ratchet or simply bend a spare screw driver.

The general principle of chuck removal is to get as much leverage as possible so that the force you exert on the chuck is maximized. In the case of a faceplate you do this by finding a piece of steel about 450 mm (18 in) long 25 mm (1 in) wide and 6 mm ($\frac{1}{4}$ in) thick and drilling two holes in it corresponding to the two opposing holes in the faceplate. You attach this piece of scrap to the faceplate by means of bolts and then exert force in the appropriate direction. You may need to strike the end with a hammer but be careful not to do this too often as you can distort the

screw holes in the faceplate. If you find that your chuck or faceplate frequently gets jammed you could resort to the old practice of using a fibre (or soft) washer between the chuck and the register of the spindle. This is not to be recommended for operations where great accuracy is required because the washer will compress during use and the chuck will not remain in exactly the same alignment.

Fig. 39
Jerry Glaser single screw chuck

Fig. 40
Cone shaped ring removed

SINGLE SCREW CHUCKS

A single screw chuck consists of a backing plate that screws onto the headstock spindle with a single screw projecting out of the centre. The object to be mounted on this must have a hole drilled in its centre so that it can be screwed onto the chuck. Naturally the thread of the screw must be cut in such a way that the rotational direction of the lathe causes the screw to tighten into the blank. On the inboard side this is like a normal screw.

You can make up your own single screw chuck by mounting a disc of wood on to a faceplate and fitting a screw into it so that it projects out of the centre for a distance of about 25 mm (1 in). I would suggest that if you try this then you should use a substantial screw such as a number 14. This must be held in the disc so that it does not rotate when the blank is turned. This can be done by drilling through the side of the disc and into the body of the screw, and putting a rod of metal in this hole.

If you are proficient at metalwork then you can make a backing plate of metal, and you can further improve the efficiency of the chuck by tapping your own screw with a parallel thread which works much better than a pointed wood screw. There are several makes of single screw chucks on the market which obviate any of this DIY activity if you can afford them. The example in **fig. 39** is made by Jerry Glaser and the cone shaped part removed in **fig. 40** reverses for smaller objects.

When holding blanks of over 250 mm (10 in) diameter I replace this disc with a wooden disc which fits over the threaded section (**fig. 41**). This shortens the projection of the screw (**fig. 42**) so that the base of the object held can be thinner, but because the area of contact between the base of the object and the backing plate is increased there is no loss of support. **Fig. 43** shows a 300 mm (12 in) platter blank on the chuck.

Fig. 41
Fitting wooden backing plate

Fig. 42
Wooden backing plate on chuck showing short screw projection

Fig. 43
300 mm (12 in) platter blank on single screw chuck

This chuck is an improvement on the faceplate because you can leave the chuck on the lathe and mount your pre-drilled blank onto it. To remove a blank all you do is stop the lathe, prevent the spindle from rotating and unscrew it. You can use it to hold a blank for turning the bottom of a bowl, and while it is on the lathe drill a hole in the base for the screw and then remount it on this to remove the inside. It does leave a hole in the base which needs to be filled, but this is better by half than the minimum number of screws that you need to hold a blank onto a faceplate. When I use this method of chucking I fill the hole with a plug drilled out of the inside of the platter after I have turned the bottom. The hole needed for the chuck is 6.5 mm (0.24 in) so I use a 7 mm (0.28 in) plug cutter, and after I have hollowed the platter, I simply bash the plug into the hole with a hammer. **Fig. 44** shows the plug next to the hole and **fig. 45** shows the result after the hole has been filled and sanded. If you get the grain to run in the right direction the fill is not very noticeable and no glue is involved.

Removal of single screw chuck

This will depend on the type of single screw chuck you have: if it is based on a faceplate, see the section above, if it is based on a combination chuck, see that section. If, however, it has a hole drilled in the side like the Glaser chuck, you should find that a rod of steel the same diameter as the hole and about 450 mm (18 in) long inserted into the hole should give you sufficient leverage to free it.

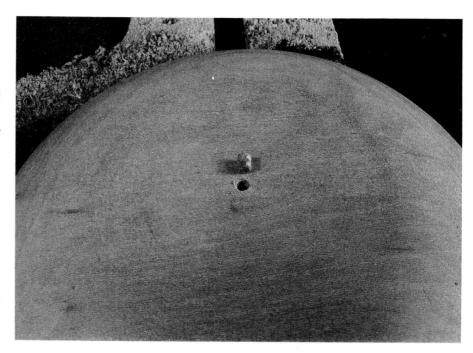

Fig. 44
Plug next to hole in base of 300 mm (12 in) platter

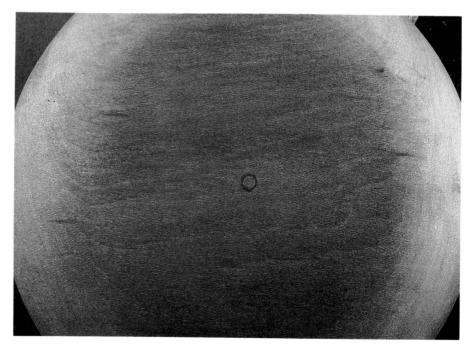

Fig. 45
Bottom after plug has been sanded

Glue

One way of overcoming the problems of screw holes is to mount the bowl in any of the above ways to turn the bottom flat, and then attach a disc of wood to the base by means of glue (thick cyanoacrylate or hot glue) with an intervening piece of paper to facilitate removal. You can then screw into this disc to attach it to a faceplate or single screw chuck rather than into the base of the bowl, or you can turn a recess into it for an expanding chuck. You need faith in the glue for this method and the bottom will need to be cleaned up after the disc has been removed.

MOUNTING BETWEEN THE CENTRES

The most low tech way to mount the bowl for turning the base is to do it between centres. This is particularly useful for blanks that are not regular, such as those that have been cut from a piece of tree with a chainsaw. It also has the great advantage that you can align the blank between the centres so that you can make the most of any feature in the wood that you wish to; perhaps to position a natural edge so that it is symmetrical. Naturally the maximum size you can turn is limited by the swing over the bed of your lathe.

When you turn the outside of the bowl between centres it is a good idea to leave a spigot on the base with the mark left by the centre in its end, so that when the bowl has been finished, either straight away or after it has dried, it can be

remounted between centres. (You may wish to remove the recess or make it circular after drying.) The hollowed end can be supported either by a specially shaped wooden blank or foam discs such as those made by Craft Supplies. See Chapter 6 on natural edge bowls for further details of this method.

EXPANDING CHUCKS

Many of the problems mentioned above can be overcome by remounting a bowl on an expanding chuck. One of the first of these to be made was the Craft Supplies Combination Chuck as in **fig. 46**, which has given me sterling service for many years. This has been superseded by the Precision Combination Chuck and chucks based on similar principles are now made by other firms such as Multistar.

Axminster Power Tools have two chucks that incorporate expanding dovetail collets. The type based on the 125 mm (5 in) four-jaw chuck can be seen in **fig. 47** – this is available in a 100 mm (4 in) version. This company has also produced a new chucking system, called the Carlton (**fig. 48**), based on a type of four-jaw chuck which does not overhang the bed as far as the standard four-jaw and is not so heavy. It is safer than the normal four-jaw because the jaws do not project so far from the body when fully expanded. The advantages over other chucks are strength of construction, amount of adjustment from a minimum diameter of 60 mm ($2\frac{3}{8}$ in) to a maximum of 90 mm ($3\frac{1}{2}$ in) and the fact that the adjustment is carried out by means of a single key rather than the two spanners required by some other chucks. The Carlton chuck can be fitted with nylon collets which can

Fig. 46
Craft Supplies combination chuck

Fig. 47
Axminster power tools system

Fig. 48
Carlton chuck with expanding dovetail
collets

be turned to your preferred diameter, and the chuck can be taken apart for cleaning.

Before you can use any expanding dovetail collet system you need to mount the bowl on the lathe by means of either a faceplate, a single screw chuck or a pin chuck so that the bottom of the bowl can be turned flat and then a recess turned for the chuck. But all the problems of remounting to hollow out the bowl encountered when using faceplates or single screw chucks are solved: centring is no longer difficult, and the depth of recess can be as shallow as 3 mm ($\frac{1}{8}$ in) for all but the biggest bowls when you are sufficiently competent not to have too many catches.

Unfortunately, you are left with a recess in the bottom of the bowl that I find interferes with the feel of the base. I like to think that I have chosen the shape of the bowl and I would not choose to have a recess in the base which feels sharp and visually interrupts the flow of the grain. This problem is overcome by rechucking the bowl, as below.

Removal of expanding chucks

Some expanding chucks are adjusted with 'C' spanners which are generally made too short. This not only means that you bark your knuckles on the bottoms of bowls but also that they do not exert much force for removing a stuck chuck. I solved this problem by bolting extension bars on the ends of the spanners as you can see in **fig. 46**. I used some odd bits of metal I had lying around which happened to be of a similar cross section to the handles of the spanners, and they have worked perfectly ever since for routine tightening and the occasional bout of stuck chuck removal.

RE-CHUCKING

To get rid of the recess left by an expanding chuck involves remounting the bowl and turning the bottom. There are several ways of doing this, the low tech method relying on being able to turn sufficient accurately to make a chuck for the bowl to be fitted in or over. When I used this method I had a selection of reject breadboard and platter blanks that I used for the purpose. I would fit the appropriately sized one on the lathe using either a single screw chuck or a faceplate and turn a recess in it the same size as the outside of the bowl. This recess needs to be slightly tapered and about 6 mm ($\frac{1}{4}$ in) deep.

The bowl is then pushed into the recess which is sufficient to hold the bowl for finishing off the bottom, provided you do not have a catch. I found that by putting the rest across the base of the bowl, as close as possible, the bowl would not go far even if it did work loose. This works well for bowls with top rims wider than the base but, if the bowl has an incurved top, the remounting blank should be in the form of a spigot that goes inside the bowl. This is not as satisfactory as the external chuck because if you push the bowl too hard onto the spigot you can split it.

This method is fairly inefficient and requires keeping a number of blanks in the workshop to cater for all the different sizes of bowl you make. I eventually realized that my workshop was full of suitable chucks, if I had but recognized them, in the form of my large stock of roughed-out bowls. I used to get orders for several 200 mm (8 in) or 250 mm (10 in) salad bowls and so on. If I started with the smallest size first, and, when I had finished them, used the next size up as a chuck, I did not have to mount anything on the lathe that I would not finish. This is quite efficient provided that you have the roughed-out bowls available and need to do a run of suitably sized bowls.

REMOUNTING WITH AN AXMINSTER CHUCK

I then heard of the Axminster chuck and realized that it provided the perfect answer to my remounting problems i.e. one chuck that is adjustable to a wide range of bowl sizes. It is based on a self-centring four-jaw chuck which can either be 200 mm (4 in) or 225 mm (5 in) diameter, the one in **fig. 47** being 225 mm (5 in). In addition to the normal internal and, as fitted in the chuck in the figure, external jaws, there are various accessories available. These include soft metal jaws, to which can be fitted wood plates, and a set of dovetail jaws that give a wider range of movement than the normal expanding chucks.

Safety measures

All four-jaw chucks constitute a source of danger over and above other chucks in that at some stage during their use, they will have four jaws projecting by a greater or lesser extent from the body. Yet the advantages for the turner outweigh the risk attached to using them – as in all aspects of turning, all you need to do is be careful and one way of doing this is to use the internal and external jaws in such a way that they project from the body of the chuck by the least possible amount. Some people cover the jaws with rubber to diminish the pain on the knuckles, but I fear that this might have the effect of dragging your knuckles onto the jaws. The wooden jaws project even further than the standard jaws so you have to be even more careful with them. There are four things to check before you start the lathe when using a four-jaw chuck:

- Is the chuck key out of the chuck?

- Is the lathe set at the correct speed?

- Are the jaws firmly held in the chuck?

- Are you standing out of the line of fire?

If you leave the chuck key in when you start the lathe it will fly off at a great speed – it is very hard.

If you start up the lathe at a high speed and you have 450 mm (18 in) diameter wooden jaws on the chuck they can disintegrate and you will not know about it until they have been stopped by something. If that something is you, you may not ever know.

When you fit a blank into the jaws at the fullest extent of their expansion it is possible that the fourth jaw is not engaged in the chuck scroll. It is best to pull the jaws before you start the lathe to make sure this is not the case.

Just in case you are careless occasionally, the best place to stand when starting the lathe is in front of it, not at right angles to the axis in line with the flight path.

Making wooden jaws

To make the wooden jaws that fit on the wood plates you must first decide how big they need to be, which of course is limited by the maximum size your lathe can turn. The diameter of the jaws expands by about 35 mm ($1\frac{1}{4}$ in) so if your maximum swing is 450 mm (18 in) the radius of the quadrants you need to cut is 450 mm minus 35 mm divided by two i.e. 205 mm (8 in). The jaws in the figures are 350 mm (14 in) diameter maximum, so I started with quadrants of 350 mm minus 35 mm divided by two, i.e. 157 mm ($6\frac{1}{4}$ in).

I suggest that you make the jaws out of 50 mm (2 in) thick, seasoned hardwood that is not prone to splitting, such as oak, ash or elm. You do not need to start with a circular blank because it will be cut into quadrants. The best way to mark these out is by making a template out of stiff card. You draw a straight line of 157 mm, construct a right angle at one end and draw a line of the same length at that angle. With a pair of compasses you can draw a quarter circle with its centre at the point where the lines meet.

This template will be used to mark the quadrant to be cut but you must remember that the purpose is to screw the metal plates to the wood and this is an operation that may be difficult to do accurately. If you are like me you will find it very difficult to screw the plates so that their right angle corresponds exactly to the right angle of the quadrants. This is easy to get over if you cut the quadrants of wood with a bit to spare and then screw on the plates. You can then mark the position of the plates, remove them and cut the quadrants exactly to size before finally screwing the plates into position. I use screws that project 13 mm ($\frac{1}{2}$ in) into the wood. Having

said all that, I have never managed to fit my metal plates exactly into the right angles of the wood jaws so that the jaws meet exactly when fully closed, but they have always worked perfectly well despite this.

Fitting the jaws to the chuck

When the plates are screwed to the quadrants (**fig. 49**) you can fit them in the Axminster chuck which is best done on the lathe (**fig. 50**). **Fig. 51** shows the quadrants expanded and **fig. 52** shows them closed. Each plate is marked with a number from one to four which corresponds to a number inside each slot in the chuck. It is a good idea to write this

Fig. 49
Quadrants screwed to jaws

Fig. 50
Wood jaws closed side view

Fig. 51
Jaws expanded

Fig. 52
Jaws closed

Fig. 53
Using ratchet spanner

Fig. 54
Recess in jaws

Fig. 55
Blank in recess

number large on the wooden jaws so that it is easy to read. The jaws are closed either by means of the provided chuck key or an adapted ratchet spanner as in **fig. 53** which enables you to avoid catching your knuckles on the back of the jaws. You should make sure that the metal jaws close completely, which may necessitate removing some wood from the joins in the wood jaws.

Once you have established that the jaws close it is a good idea to turn a recess in the jaws (**fig. 54**) as deep as the screws in the plates allow and about 150 mm (6 in) in diameter. The purpose of this is so that when you expand the jaws to their maximum you can insert a circular blank (about 180 mm ($7\frac{1}{4}$ in)) to tighten them onto (**fig. 55**). This enables you to be quite sure that each time you expand the jaws to measure the maximum expansion you do so to exactly the same point. It is not a good idea to use the jaws at the very outer limit of their possible expansion in case they do work loose. The blank has no function once the steps in the jaws have been finished.

Turning the recess

The tools I use to turn the recess and the steps are a 12.5 mm ($\frac{1}{2}$ in) bowl turning gouge (with the bevel ground back) to remove the bulk of the wood (**fig. 56**), and a square ended scraper, as used for the recesses for expanding chucks, to turn the sides of the steps which should overhang slightly (**fig. 57**).

When the jaws are expanded as far as is safe you can draw a line to

Fig. 56
Using gouge to turn out step

Fig. 57
Using scraper to cut side of step

mark the outer edge of the largest step. The outer edge of the jaws is not circular when expanded, but with a bit of trial and error you can mark with a pencil the minimum thickness of the outer lip which should be about 13 mm ($\frac{1}{2}$ in).

If you now close the jaws you can turn the recess for the widest step almost up to the inside of the pencil mark, which since it is not now circular, appears as just a blur. I make the steps about 6.25 mm ($\frac{1}{4}$ in) deep and slightly overhung. The widest step (when contracted) of the jaws in the figure has a diameter of 300 mm (12 in), but it is important for you to measure the diameter of your step so that when you expand the jaws you can mark the diameter of the next step down

to give yourself full coverage of all possible diameters.

Having made this measurement you expand the jaws, insert the 180 mm blank, tighten the jaws onto it and measure the maximum size of the step, which in the case of the one in the figures was 335 mm (13.4 in). The next step should cover the minimum size of the first step, i.e. be slightly more than 300 mm (12 in) so you expand the jaws and mark this with a pencil as above. You then contract the jaws and turn this step as before and continue to expand and contract the jaws measuring and turning steps until you reach the bottom of the first recess you turned, deeper than which it is not safe to go. You can see finished jaws in use in **figs.**

89–90, page 68; the jaws being made in **figs. 49–57** have four steps from a minimum contracted diameter of 235 mm (9.5 in) and the gap between each step was 15.6 mm ($\frac{5}{8}$ in).

Removal of Axminster chuck

If you have large wooden jaws on your four-jaw chuck you should have sufficient diameter available to free the chuck if it should get stuck, but if you are only using the ordinary internal or external jaws you should be able to free the chuck by gripping a bar or piece of pipe between the jaws at right angles to the axis of the lathe and using this as a lever.

−5

TURNING SIMPLE BOWLS

In the course of this project I describe in detail the tool techniques needed to make a simple bowl, in this case a salad bowl. I also describe how it is possible to use unseasoned wood for this purpose and the reasons why this is desirable.

CHOOSING WOOD

The type of timber that you can use for salad bowls can be any hardwood that is free of knots and shakes and does not have a strong smell. Suitable species include ash, which I use a lot because the colour and grain (particularly of olive ash) are so attractive, sycamore or maple, which are the traditional timbers, elm, if you can get hold of it, and oak or any of the fruitwoods if they can be found large enough. It is not enough, however, to know that a species of timber is suitable, for the quality of the timber varies from tree to tree and even within the same plank. Experience is the best guide in these matters but beware of unusually lightweight planks for the timber may have gone 'sleepy', i.e. rotten and too soft to be of any use.

Seasoning

One of the problems of working wood is that, when felled, the medium contains large quantities of water which proceed to evaporate in response to the relative dryness of the surrounding atmosphere (see pages 20–21 for more explanation). The problem of tensions caused by this evaporation is minimized by felling trees when they are dormant and contain the minimum water, but the water content still needs reducing in a way that lessens the cracking caused by the volume change. One way of doing this is to cut the log into planks and to stack them on bearers with slats between each plank in a shed that allows the air to circulate but keeps off the rain.

This works well with planks up to 50 mm (2 in) thick which on average take one year for each inch of thickness to dry to 18 per cent water content, but for thicker planks such as those required for a salad bowl (100 mm (4 in)) this method has disadvantages. For a start you have to have a lot of storage space to keep the planks for the requisite time and furthermore the thickness means that the differences of water content in different parts of the plank create a build-up of tension which can result in a lot of cracking. Air drying is also inadequate in the climate of Great Britain for wooden items intended for use in a centrally-heated environment where the relative humidity is very low and timber is only stable if it has a moisture content of 12 per cent or lower.

It is possible to buy wood that has been artificially dried to the correct water content but this is an expensive process that needs to be done properly to avoid the problems of honeycombing (where the cell structure degrades) and case hardening, where the outer layers are dried but the inside remains damp.

You can find out the water content of wood with a moisture meter if you can afford one, but do make sure that you insert the probes into the centre of the wood, which is the dampest part, by cutting a slice off the end of the plank. If you do not have a meter you can ascertain the water content by the following process. Cut a thin sample of the wood at least 23 mm (9 in) from the end of the plank and weigh it, write the date of weighing and the weight on the sample and leave it to dry in a warm, dry place for a fortnight or so. If you are in a hurry you can put it in the oven at no more than 100°C. You will be able to tell if it is dry by weighing it at intervals; when the weight stays the same the sample has lost all the water it is going to. If you work out the difference between the dry weight and the wet weight in percentage terms you will have the original water content. So, if the first weight was 8 units and the dry weight 7 units, then the water content is $\frac{1}{7}$ or approximately 14 per cent.

TURNING WET WOOD

There are two approaches to dealing with wood that is not dry enough, both of which use the wood before it has had a chance to degrade:

- Turn the wood to a finish while it is wet and to allow the bowl to distort but prevent it cracking by turning it thin (see Chapter 6).

- Turn the bowl roughly to the shape required but with thicker walls and leave it to dry.

If you do want a bowl that is completely stable it is a good idea to rough it out and leave it for a week or two, even if it has the right water content, because that way you allow the tensions in the wood to work their way out before finishing it.

Re-turning

When a roughed out bowl distorts after being left to dry, it will need

remounting on the lathe before it can be re-turned. If you used a faceplate to mount it, it is possible to use the old screw holes provided that your original screw holes were aligned along the grain because wood contracts more across the grain than along it when drying. That is assuming that you will only use two screws in the faceplate which, with a little experience, should be all that is necessary. If you find that after drying the base is no longer flat, the faceplate will not support the bowl securely and it will be necessary to plane the base flat either with a hand plane or an electric one.

If you supported the bowl on an expanding chuck, the recess in the base will probably be elliptical after drying, in which event the chuck will neither fit nor get sufficient grip. I have found that if the wood was not too wet when roughed out I can often remount the bowl in a slightly distorted hole using the Axminster expanding jaws, because they are made of solid steel and can exert greater pressure in the recess than the more fragile jaws of the Craft Supplies expanding chuck. There is also a greater range of movement in the Axminster jaws which means that you can make the original recess just a bit larger than the minimum to allow for contraction during drying. If, however, the hole is very distorted it is safer to remount the bowl and re-turn the recess.

Drying roughed out bowls

To speed up the process of drying you can put the roughed out bowl

in a dry, warm atmosphere but beware of trying to dry the wood too fast as this may cause it to split. Just as in the plank, splits are most likely to occur on the end grain and the answer to this problem is the same: seal the end grain with glue, emulsified paraffin wax or paint. End grain occurs on two sides of the bowl in a straight-grained sample but where the grain is wild or the wood burred, end grain can occur anywhere and needs sealing. A word of warning about the use of paint: I used some old white paint to seal some burr bowls when I started to use this method forgetting that it was likely to penetrate into the burrs. I only did it once.

If you only have a few bowls to dry, you will probably be able to find sufficient space in the house, but if you are into mass production you may find it economical to invest in a domestic de-humidifier and install it in a sealed, insulated cupboard (**fig. 58**). I made one of these in the corner of a shed using timber for the frame and lining it with a sandwich of polythene, expanded polystyrene, chipboard and more polythene and installed slatted shelves on which I put my roughed out bowls open side down so that the air circulates freely.

I also use this 'kiln' to dry platter blanks but I always seal the edges of these to prevent splitting. The shrinkage across the grain can be quite dramatic in these so you need to cut them larger than the size you want the finished article by a factor that varies with the water content. In the kiln you should separate each blank from the next with sticks or by standing them on their edges.

Fig. 58
Framework of drying shed – to be
insulated with polythene, expanded
polystyrene and chipboard

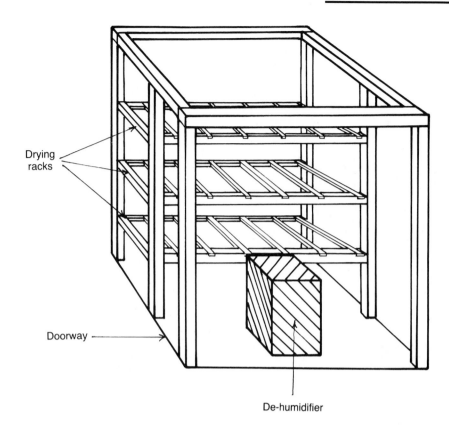

Drying
racks

Doorway

De-humidifier

TURNING A SALAD BOWL

The base

The blank can be any width from
about 150 mm (6 in) up to 450 mm
(18 in) but does need to be at least
100 mm (4 in) deep so that the salad
can be tossed without scattering too
many lettuce leaves over the floor.
A bowl 150 mm (6 in) × 100 mm
(4 in) is usually used as a side salad
bowl and bowls upwards of 200 mm
(8 in) across are usually used to toss
salads in. They can both be mounted
by any of the methods described in
'chucking' but I tend to do the
smallest size in a different way to
the others because the base needs to
be smaller than 125 mm (5 in) to be
in proportion and the fact that it is
so small enables the use of

techniques that are unsuitable for
larger bowls.

The speed you set the lathe at will
depend on the size of blank and
your experience. There are no hard
and fast rules about lathe speed but
if you are in any doubt start slow
and speed up as and when you feel
confident (see page 16 for
recommended speeds). If you are
not familiar with the tool, work out
how to use it by holding it against
the work before you start the lathe
and see how the tool can be held so
that the bevel rubs on the wood.
You can rotate the work by hand to
see if the way you are holding the
tool will produce a shaving.

Where possible you should turn
towards the centre of the work so
that you are working against the
natural tendency of centrifugal

force to throw the tool outwards
and you should cut so that the fibres
of the wood you are cutting are
supported by the fibres underneath.

Chucking

In the case of side salad bowls I do
the base on a single screw chuck
(**fig. 34, page 39 and fig. 59**) and
I form a spigot on the base as in **fig.
60**, and then hollow out on a four-
jaw chuck or the spigot collets of the
Carlton chuck (**figs. 61–62**). This
particular ash blank had a small
shake in the side, circled with pencil
(**fig. 59**), which I hoped would be
turned away when the sides were
shaped but my optimism was
misplaced and, as so often happens
with this type of shake, it kept right
on going into the wood and the

Fig. 59
Side salad bowl being mounted on single
screw chuck

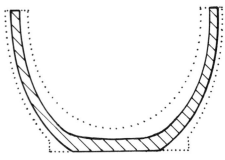

Fig. 60
Position of finished side salad bowl within
roughed out blank with spigot

Fig. 61
Carlton chuck with spigot collets

Fig. 62
Side salad bowl held in Carlton chuck

Fig. 63
Side salad bowl remounted in four-jaw
chuck expanding collets

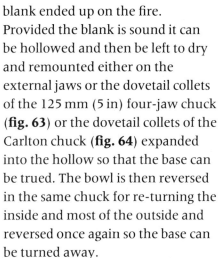

blank ended up on the fire.
Provided the blank is sound it can
be hollowed and then be left to dry
and remounted either on the
external jaws or the dovetail collets
of the 125 mm (5 in) four-jaw chuck
(**fig. 63**) or the dovetail collets of the
Carlton chuck (**fig. 64**) expanded
into the hollow so that the base can
be trued. The bowl is then reversed
in the same chuck for re-turning the
inside and most of the outside and
reversed once again so the base can
be turned away.

Bowls up to 300 mm (12 in)
across can be mounted on a single
screw chuck to turn the bottom but
larger than this I tend to use a
faceplate, sometimes with as many
as four screws in if it is very big. **Fig.
65** shows a 300 mm (12 in) ×
100 mm (4 in) lacewood or London

Fig. 64
Side salad bowl remounted in Carlton
dovetail collets

Fig. 65
Lacewood 300 mm (12 in) × 100 mm (4 in)
blank on single screw chuck

Fig. 66
Turning base with square ended 12.5 mm
($\frac{1}{2}$ in) gouge

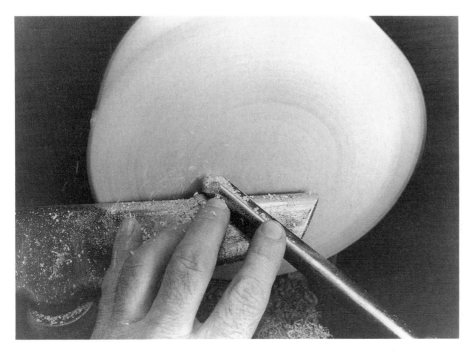

Fig. 67
Smoothing cut with ground back 12.5 mm
($\frac{1}{2}$ in) gouge

plane blank mounted on a single screw and you can see that I have made the most of the wood by incorporating the waney edge where the rounded side of the bowl will be.

I like to true up the base of the bowl first with the square ended 12.5 mm ($\frac{1}{2}$ in) gouge (**fig. 66**). You cut from the outside to the middle and with the flute of the gouge pointing in the direction of the cut. The part of the edge that does the cutting should be between the centre and the end of the right-hand side but nearer the centre. This is the side of the tool that is nearest the rest.

When you have worked out the angle at which the tool cuts cleanly, you can see that this angle should be maintained across the whole of the face to be turned. This is done by supporting the tool at the rest with which ever hand you prefer, the handle with your other hand and the end of the handle against your hip or side and moving the tool across the face of the work by transferring your weight from one foot to the other, not by just moving your hands (see **figs. 79–80**). If you practise this before you start the lathe you should be able to do the cut smoothly.

When you have got rid of the roughness of the base you can do a smoothing cut with the same size, ground back gouge working outwards with the flute pointing up (**fig. 67**). This is a very fine cut and the bevel must rub or a catch will result. Centrifugal force has no effect on this cut because it is so fine and the edge is nearly parallel to the diameter of the blank.

Rounding the sides

A true base gives you a level surface on which to rest the tool bevel for rounding the sides of the bowl (**fig. 68**). There is usually no need to true up the sides of the bowl before shaping and indeed this is a difficult cut because you have to start without the bevel rubbing. The end grain can also be difficult to cut cleanly when the blank is not perfectly round. As you proceed with the shaping of the sides it is important to keep the tool rest close to the surface so that the tool tip is not a long way from its support, which can cause flexing of the tool shaft. It is also safer to stop the lathe when moving the rest to prevent it from catching on the rotating bowl.

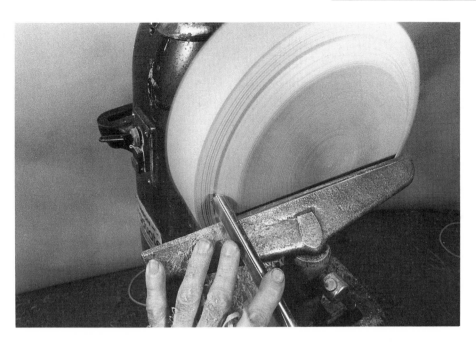

Fig. 68
Rounding side of bowl with straight across gouge

Preparing for the chuck

The bottom of the bowl has to be prepared for whatever means you have for remounting it. If you are to use a single screw chuck you should drill a hole in the base with a suitably sized drill bit held in a drill but using the power of the lathe, provided it is rotating in the appropriate direction. If you are going to screw a faceplate directly onto the base you should mark the centre with a pencil, but it is difficult to accurately screw on the faceplate. This leaves you with two choices:

- You accept this inaccuracy and do not finish the outside of the bowl at this stage – this will only work if you can get your rest around the back of the bowl when re-mounted (**fig. 69**).

Fig. 69
Cutting outside of bowl around the back

- You fit a 12.5 mm ($\frac{1}{2}$ in) thick disc of wood on the faceplate and turn a 3 mm ($\frac{1}{8}$ in) spigot on this to act as a register for a recess in the base of the bowl. This will enable the bowl to be accurately positioned so that you can screw through the disc into the base.

If you do not mind having the recess in the bottom that an expanding chuck requires, you can turn this recess now or you can avoid any marks in the bottom by gluing a disc of wood to the base with a sheet of paper between the base and disc (to make it easier to remove) and turn a recess in this or prepare it for screwing on the faceplate.

To turn a recess in the base of a bowl for an expanding chuck you must first of all mark the appropriate diameter. I use a pair of dividers for this while the work is rotating, but if you want a pre-set low tech alternative a couple of nails in a strip of wood work just as well provided you do not lose the device in a pile of shavings and sit on it.

You can either set the device of your choice to half the diameter of the recess and line one point up with the centre while marking the diameter, in which case you can engage both points at once; or you can set the device at the full diameter and put one point in to do the marking while you check that it is in place with the other point (**fig. 116, page 83**). It is not wise to engage both points in this latter case as this can put a permanent knot in your dividers.

The recess can be hollowed with a gouge but the edges need to be overhung for the expanding jaws to fit in. This is best done with a square ended scraper (**fig. 70**) ground so that the top left hand corner is about 85° instead of 90°, which naturally produces a dovetail when pushed straight in. If you intend to leave the recess then it can be sanded at this stage but be careful not to sand the walls of the recess as differential sanding can make them elliptical and not such a good fit for the dovetail collets.

Hollowing

Fig. 71 shows the blank being mounted on the dovetail collets of the Carlton chuck, but it could just as easily be any of the expanding chucks detailed in Chapter 4, pages 45–47. I like to tighten up the collets so that the bowl is just supported and then rotate the chuck by hand to see if the blank is centred before giving the collets a final tightening.

When you have remounted the bowl you must first true up the top with a gouge to make sure that there are no faults in the wood that you wish to remove. If you finished the outside when turning the bottom and are happy with the shape when the blank is remounted you will obviously not need to do anything more to the outside, but if you did not finish the outside or want to alter the shape it is best to do this before you hollow the inside.

When the top has been trued up you can measure the depth of the blank with a ruler across the base and another down the side so that you know how deep you can hollow. I like to drill a hole inside the bowl at this stage so that when I am hollowing I can keep the hole in view and when it disappears stop hollowing. It also stops a cone forming at the centre of the bottom which can be quite tricky to get rid of. To do the drilling I use the tool in the basic kit (**fig. 1, page 12**) which is simply a drill bit in a tool handle. I mark the depth with my thumb on the bit and push it in, removing it frequently to get rid of the shavings.

For your first few bowls it may be necessary to establish the lip with a straight scraper as in **fig. 72**. This stops the gouge from skating across the bowl should you get the angle of cut wrong.

Remember that it is the lathe that provides the power for the cut, not you. Provided that the tool is sharp and you present it at the correct angle you should not have to force the tool. If you do find that you are having to push hard then check that the tool is sharp and if it is (and you still need to use a lot of force) adjust the angle at which you are holding it. This is a difficult process to describe accurately because the difference between holding the tool at the correct angle and getting it wrong enough to cause the tool to chatter is so slight.

I use a 12.5 mm ($\frac{1}{2}$ in) square ended gouge to remove the bulk of the wood, as in **fig. 73**. For the first few cuts the tool passes at the same angle across the front of the bowl but as you get deeper you will find that in order to keep the bevel rubbing the tool should describe an arc within the bowl as in **fig. 74** and in the sequence of **figs. 75–78**.

These figures show the course of the tool, but what they do not show is that normally when I hollow a

Fig. 70
Cutting overhang of dovetail recess with scraper

Fig. 71
Mounting blank on Carlton chuck

Fig. 72
Establishing lip with straight scraper

Fig. 73
Hollowing with straight across gouge

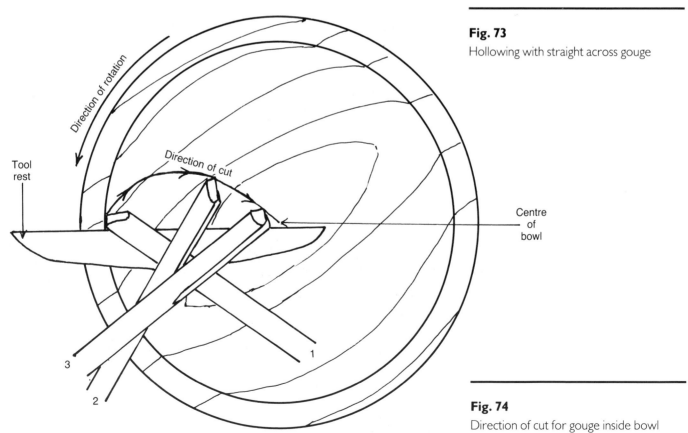

Fig. 74
Direction of cut for gouge inside bowl

Fig. 75
Start of cut with straight across gouge

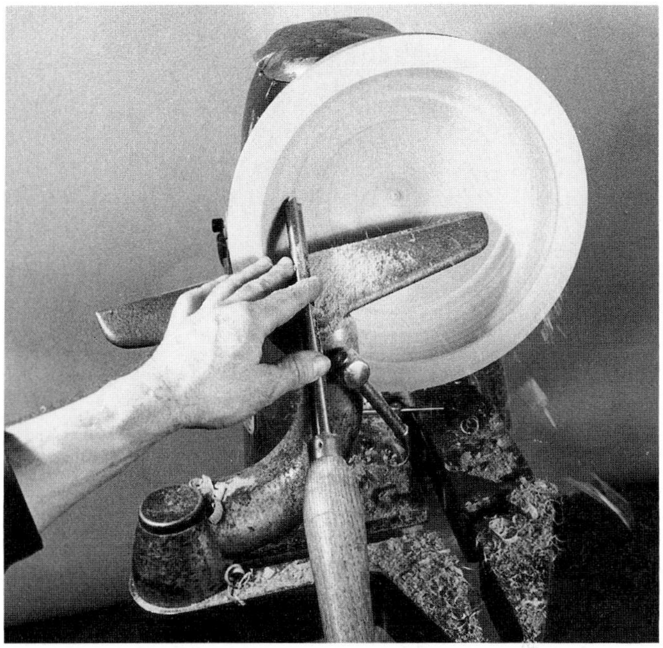

Fig. 76
Part way along cut

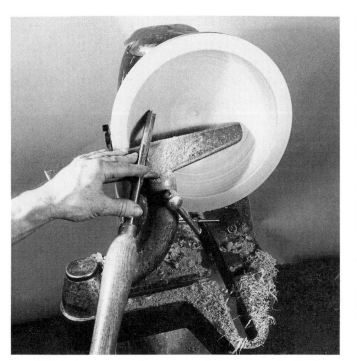

Fig. 77
Next stage in cut

Fig. 78
Cut at centre

bowl my right hand is pressed against my right thigh (**figs. 9–12, pages 16–17**). This provides extra support for the tool which can then be directed not simply by moving the hand but also by transferring the weight from the right foot to the left (**figs. 79–80**).

When the bowl is nearly as deep as possible the square ended gouge becomes difficult to manoeuvre to keep the bevel rubbing, particularly in the sharpest part of the curve where the side merges into the bottom. To illustrate this point I have used a cut away ash bowl (**figs. 81–82**) which, although it is not as steeply curved as many bowls are, shows that at this point the square ended gouge (**fig. 81**) has to be held at such an angle that the part supported by the rest (the fulcrum) is further from the bowl surface than with the ground back gouge (**fig. 83**). This problem is even worse if you are using a straight tool rest (**fig. 84**) as opposed to the curved one (**figs. 87–88**) and this makes the square ended more difficult to control at this stage. The ground back gouge also has the advantage of having a shorter bevel which enables it to get into tighter curves than the square ended gouge.

The curved rest in the figure is made by Craft Supplies and has the advantage of being reversible so that it can be used on the outboard side of the lathe. It can also be used with other accessories. If you do not want to go to the expense of buying such

Fig. 79
Weight on right foot

Fig. 80
Weight on left foot

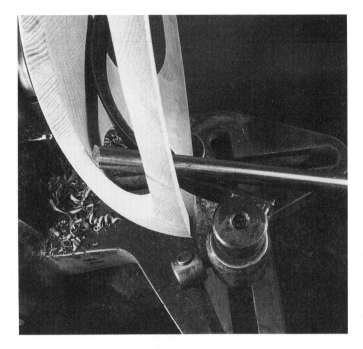

Fig. 81
Square ended gouge inside bowl

Fig. 82
Ground back gouge inside bowl

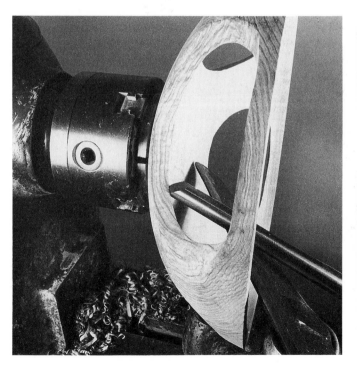

Fig. 83
Ground back gouge on straight rest

Fig. 84
Square ended gouge on straight rest

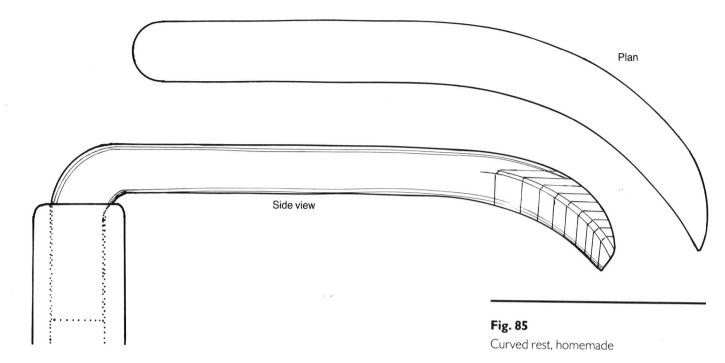

Plan

Side view

Fig. 85
Curved rest, homemade

a rest and are familiar with metalwork it is quite feasible to bend a steel bar of the diameter to fit your rest arm into a curve. Even I, a complete novice at metalwork, have been able to make one that has a curve at the end of a straight section so that I can get the rest support in very close even when doing a bowl as deep as 250 mm (10 in) (**fig. 85 and fig. 122, page 86**). Another simple modification of the rest is to drill and tap an extra hole in the rest arm so that the lever which tightens the rest is not in the way of the bowl (**fig. 86**). I have also replaced the lever with a wooden one (**figs. 11–12, page 17**) which is easier to tighten: first, it is longer, and second, because it is made of wood, it can be struck with the tool handle without serious damage.

Fig. 87 shows the angle of the ground back gouge at the top of the wall with the bevel clearly rubbing, and **fig. 88** shows the same gouge at the centre of the bottom.

Fig. 86
Extra hole in rest support

Fig. 87
Angie of ground back gouge, top of wall

Fig. 88
Angle of ground back gouge bottom of
bowl

Fig. 89
300 mm (12 in) ash bowl in Axminster
wood jaws

Fig. 90
Same bowl in same jaws from the side

Roughing out

If the wood is not dry enough to be
stable in the conditions in which it
will be used (12 per cent moisture
content is a safe figure to aim at) or
you want to leave the bowl to allow
the natural tensions in it to express
themselves, you should leave the
walls thicker than they will be when
finished (about 10 per cent of the
width of the bowl) and remove the
bowl to the drying shed (see page
55 and **fig. 58**).

After the wood has dried you will
need to remount the bowl. If the
original support was by means of an
expanding chuck the recess may not
be circular any more, in which case
you can remount the bowl by any of
the ways in **fig. 36**, page 40. If the
bowl has distorted a great deal then
you may have to use some hot melt
glue to add extra support in
methods **b** and **c**, and if you use the
Axminster wood plates you may
need to plane the top of the bowl
flat to get sufficient purchase. **Figs.
89–90** show a roughed out and
dried 150 mm (16 in) ash bowl
mounted in the wood plate jaws of
the Axminster chuck and ready for
turning the bottom flat and the
recess to the correct size.

When the dried, roughed out
bowl has had its recess corrected it
can then be mounted in the
expanding dovetail collets and the
warpage can be turned away using
the same techniques that are used in
turning a bowl from scratch.

As the bowl deepens it is
important to get a good finish on the
top part of the inside, particularly if
the bowl is thin, because the sides
tend to flex away from the tool. You

should make sure that the walls are the required thickness by frequently stopping the lathe and checking them either with callipers or by finger and thumb when you are confident of using this method. You can check that the depth is right by placing one ruler across the top and another down the middle to the bottom.

When the required depth and wall thickness have been achieved it is useful to do a finishing cut in the bottom (**fig. 91**) with the gouge on its side and working from the centre outwards. It is only possible to turn the bottom with the bevel in contact as far as the point where the side and bottom meet, but you get a smoother cut with this cut than going inwards because the edge that is cutting is longer. It is not an easy cut to master, however, because if the bevel support is too far away a nasty catch can result.

On the inside of the walls I do a finishing cut with the 6.25 mm ($\frac{1}{4}$ in) gouge (**fig. 125, page 88**) to get rid of any roughness as the thin section of this tool can take such a sharp edge. The cuts down the sides are the same as with the 13 mm ($\frac{1}{2}$ in) gouge only gentler, but on the bottom you can cut outwards with the side of this tool.

You should be able to get a good finish from this tool but if the grain is a little unruly you may need to apply some cooking oil or water (whichever is compatible with your finish) to the rough spots and then take off a fine sliver with the fine gouge. The oil soaks into the rough areas and they are easier to cut as a result. The decision about how long you should persist with the tool

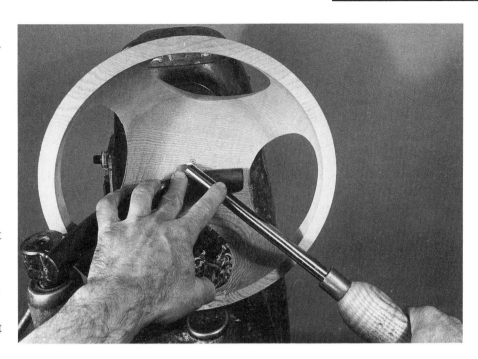

Fig. 91
Finishing cut in bottom of bowl with ground back gouge

Fig. 92
Finishing cut with scraper pointing down

before resorting to sandpaper is a matter of experience and patience, but you should certainly aim to get rid of most rough spots with the tool because sandpaper is expensive and creates harmful dust, while excessive sanding can make the surface uneven.

I also use a 37.5 mm ($1\frac{1}{2}$ in) half round scraper to do a smoothing cut inside bowls but not the walls where the end grain can easily cause the tool to catch. I use the tool in the bottom either in the traditional way with the cutting edge below the level of the rest (which should be set slightly above centre height as in **fig. 92**) or with a shearing cut which gives a finer finish if you can master it (**fig. 8, page 14**).

FINISHING

When you are quite sure that you have obtained as good a finish from the tool as you can then you will need to sand the bowl. Hand held abrasives are the cheapest way of doing this (see Chapter 1, page 18), but power sanding is quicker.

Power sanding

For power sanding you need an electric drill (preferably two speed with reverse) and I would suggest a 600 watt tool because the drill has to be able to work against the power of the lathe motor. The actual sanding is done by abrasive discs attached to foam pads and the best method of attachment is by velcro. It is possible to use adhesive pads but the dust and heat tend to make the sticking unreliable. The pads are available in a range of diameters from 25 mm (1 in) through 50 mm (2 in) to 75 mm (3 in). For bowl turning the two biggest sizes are the best.

When power sanding you work through a range of grit sizes, as with hand sanding, and you can either leave the pad in the drill and change over the discs as you move to a finer grade or you can have pads dedicated to each grit size and remove the pads to change the grade. I use the latter method because the velcro loses its adhesiveness if you continually remove it from the pad. You should be able to develop the knack of removing and inserting the pads without using a chuck key by working against the inertia of the drill. You do this by holding your hand around the chuck when starting the drill to tighten it up and loosening it by stopping the drill and rotating the chuck and drill in the opposite directions with a jerk. While you are sanding you will need to keep your fingers loosely around the chuck so that if it works loose you can contract them and cause the chuck to tighten.

The angle at which the pads should be presented can be seen in the section on natural edge bowls (**figs. 126–127**). It is important not to have the lathe going too fast and to use the drill at a fairly slow speed because the discs are not as effective at the very high speeds you can get by combining the two. You should also avoid pressing too hard on the pads because this can cause heat build up which can melt the glue that holds the velcro in place.

The edge of the disc that contacts the work should naturally be the one that is rotating in the opposite direction to the work and it is very important to keep the disc moving over the surface as a disc can remove a lot of wood in a short time if you leave it in one place. I generally go over the whole of the surface with 80 grit for as long as I think necessary before stopping the lathe to see if all rough spots have gone. I then work on the rough spots with the work stationary. You have to be very careful when doing this not to sand out too much of a hollow, so again the answer is to keep the disc moving. You should be able to hold the work with one hand while holding the drill with the other hand at the angle required to keep it more or less under control, but this may take some practice.

After you have removed a rough spot with the work stationary, you will need to use the same grit on the rotating work to get rid of the marks left by the disc before graduating to the next grade. I find that 80 grit gets rid of the rough grain on most bowls and that 120 grit will remove the marks left by that. You can progress to 180 grit and even to 220 and 320 but I have strong doubts as to the effectiveness of the finest grades which seem to lose their cut very quickly presumably because the small particles of grit rapidly get hot and melt. It is more effective and cheap to use hand held 220 grit after 180 grit discs.

Finishes

I always use cooking oil and wax to finish bowls which are going to come into contact with food, because they are non-toxic. See Chapter 3, page 32.

Remounting

It will depend on how you held the bowl on the lathe as to whether you will need to remount the bowl to clean up the bottom. I refer you to the chapter on chucking for the various methods you can use. If you do choose to use wooden jaws on the Axminster chuck it is a good idea to put a piece of cloth on the edge in contact with the jaws to prevent it from being marked (**fig. 96**).

The purpose of remounting is to make the bottom of the bowl look as you want it to, which may involve removing all trace of the chucking system (if there is enough thickness of wood on the bottom) or just rounding off the sides of the recess so that the hard edge is no longer there to interfere with the smooth feel of the bowl (**fig. 93**). You can see that the flow of the grain can easily be seen while leaving both the interest of the hollow in the bottom and the effect of the play of light on the surface.

You may wish to add ornamentation to the outside as

Fig. 93
Bottom of burr elm bowl with rounded recess

Fig. 94
Turning groove with fluted parting tool

Fig. 95
Turning left of groove with same tool

Fig. 96
Ash bowl with grooves finished

described on page 31 and shown in **fig. 28**. The way this was done can be seen in **figs. 94–96**. The chuck used is the Axminster four-jaw with wood plates as described in Chapter 4, page 48. The tool to use is the fluted parting tool intended for spindle work – this requires great delicacy in this context where the grain is in an unfavourable direction twice per revolution and the bevel is not supporting the edge. Move the tool from side to side to develop the rounded profile in the middle of the groove – the finish you can obtain is so good that no sanding is required, indeed if you sand such fine details you are certain to lose definition.

Of course, this is not the only tool you can use to add decoration to the outside of the bowl – it depends on the shape of the detail you wish to add. The only limitation to the ornamentation you can add to the bottom of a bowl using this type of chuck is your imagination and skill, the amount of wood you have left and the fact that you cannot touch the top 12.5 mm ($\frac{1}{2}$ in) because it is in the chuck.

6

NATURAL EDGE BOWLS

The beauty of bowls with an edge comprised of either bark or the natural edge under the bark is that you are in no doubt that they are made from naturally occurring material. The problem about making such a bowl is that because the top is irregular and you wish to preserve its natural form (at least at the rim) you do not have the same range of mounting options as you do with an ordinary bowl.

Some of the effects that you can achieve can be seen in **figs. 97–100** and **figs. 19–20**, page 27. **Fig. 97** is a natural edge boxwood bowl turned green with the bark left on and measuring approximately 100 mm (4 in) across. **Fig. 98** shows a natural edge burr elm bowl measuring approximately 275 mm (11 in) across with the bark removed (actually it fell off because it was rotten) and **fig. 99** shows a yew bowl 125 mm (5 in) across with the waney edge top and bottom. I have never before or since had a piece of wood that had the potential for this sort of bowl but I am pleased that I saw the chance when I came to use the wood. **Fig. 100** shows the laburnum bowl featured in this chapter while **fig. 20** is a burr oak bowl rough turned and allowed to dry.

CHOOSING WOOD

Making bowls with a natural edge allows you to experiment with any type of wood available and it is very often free. There is no harm in trying anything you can get; indeed the fact that the bowl has an unusually shaped top can sometimes mitigate the fact that the timber itself is not particularly attractive. The commonest source of such timber is relatively small trees, perhaps from a garden, and you can make very attractive small bowls from such wood.

Another source that you could tap is the offcut pile of a sawmill, or, if you are a user of large quantities of wood as I am and have trees planked to order, you can have the outside slabs of the logs left thicker than usual and cut your blanks from these.

If you have a small tree to use for natural edge bowls and the wood is freshly felled it is best to use it soon because this type of wood is very prone to splitting. If you cannot use

Fig. 97
Boxwood bowl wet turned with bark on

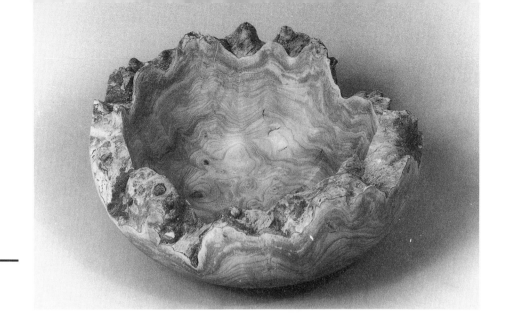

Fig. 98
Burr elm bowl natural top without bark

Fig. 99
Yew bowl natural top double ended

Fig. 100
Laburnum bowl natural top wet turned

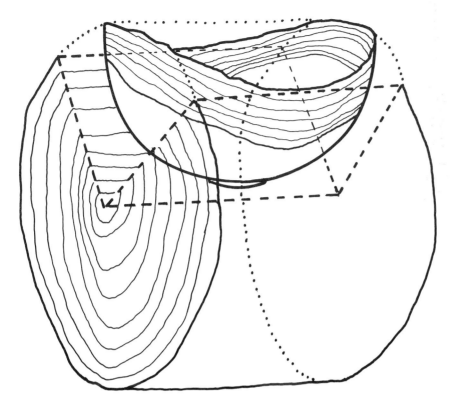

it soon it is a good idea to leave it in as long a length as possible, seal the ends and keep it out of the sun (see Chapter 2, page 21). The most cost effective way of cutting it is like a cake (**figs. 101–103**). You will reduce the amount of splitting by first working out the best way of getting the bowls you want from it, and then splitting it down the heart, because the shakes that emanate from the heart will be prevented by this. If you cannot decide how you will use it, it is best to split it in half which also has the effect of reducing the chance of shakes.

Fig. 101
Natural top bowl out of log

Fig. 102
End of log marked out for bowl, rotten section at top

Fig. 103
Other end of log

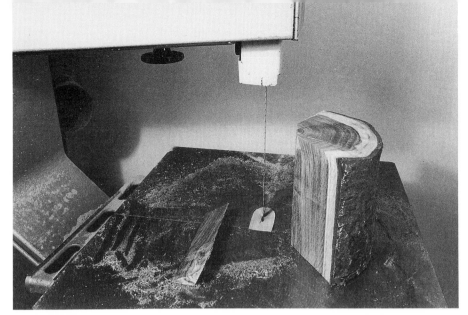

Preparing blanks

Splitting can be done with wedges or you can use a chainsaw (bearing in mind the dangers inherent in using this tool, see Chapter 1, page 12). If you have a bandsaw you could use this if it has sufficient depth of cut. In **figs. 102–103** you can see the two ends of a laburnum log marked out to avoid the rotten section in the top half of **fig. 102**. When I have cut a length of log into segments (**fig. 104**) I like to cut a flat surface where the segments used to meet at the centre of the tree: this provides a flat surface on which to stand the segment when cutting it round, and also gives a flat surface in which to engage the tailstock centre of the lathe.

It is not too difficult to mark a circle on the surface of a smooth log using a pair of dividers (**fig. 105**). As you can see in the figure, the overhangs of the blank are supported by wedges glued into place with hot melt glue to stop it tilting over when being sawn. I just used pieces of offcuts from the log and simply cut through them when cutting out the blank (**fig. 106**).

Fig. 104
Laburnum log split on bandsaw

Fig. 105
Marking circle with dividers

Fig. 106
Circular blank cut out

When you cut the blank you will be able to decide whether to leave the bark on the top. This can be very decorative as in the case of the laburnum (**figs. 102–106**) where the bark is a different colour to the sapwood, but you may have no choice in the matter if the bark is loose. This seems to depend on the species concerned, the time of year it was felled and whether you damage it. If the bark is missing in places it looks better to remove it all, but if it is simply loose in one or two patches you can glue it back with cyanoacrylate and the join should not show. In the case of the laburnum the bark stayed on for a while but as it dried it distorted and eventually had to be removed.

When the piece of timber you have is like the one in **figs. 107–108** (which is burr lime) it requires a different approach compared to a length of log. This is how the burr appeared after having been sliced off the tree which was blown down in a gale. It had no flat bottom to rest on while being bandsawn, so to make it sit level while I planed the base, I put it on a roughed out bowl of the correct size (as **fig. 109** but the other way up).

One common problem with natural edged blanks like this is that it is not so easy to draw a circle on the top of the blank because of the unevenness of the surface. One answer is to cut a circle of the required diameter out of cardboard and place this on the top of the blank which you then cut around. If the top is too uneven to do this it is not a good idea to scratch the surface as you would with dividers, for two reasons. First, because it is

Fig. 107
Piece of burr lime

Fig. 108
Side view of lime

Fig. 109
Marking top with end-grain sealer

not very visible on a rough surface, and second, because if you happen to turn it so that the mark does not exactly coincide with the outside of the bowl, you might leave a scratch on the top which is difficult, if not impossible, to remove. In the case of this particular blank I put a roughed out bowl of the correct size on top and painted end-grain sealer around it (**fig. 109**). The great advantage of doing this is that the sealer shows up white until it dries but becomes transparent after a short time. Because it consists of paraffin wax it can be buffed up to a good matt finish with a nylon brush held in an electric drill after the bowl is finished.

The options available for such a natural edge blank are either to turn it immediately with thin walls and let it warp as it dries (as in the laburnum and boxwood bowls) or to rough it out as described in the salad bowl section and then dry it and re-turn it. I tend to rough turn burr blanks because I prefer a burr bowl to be fairly chunky and I turn small bits of log thinly because the resultant warping adds to the appearance of a small bowl.

CHUCKING

The three options for the initial chucking of this type of bowl are:

- Faceplate
- Pin chuck
- Between the centres

Faceplate (**fig. 35b, page 40**)

If you can plane the bottom flat you can screw a faceplate to it. This works very well if the wood available is quite thick because this allows you to leave an extra thick bottom which can be removed to leave no screw holes. Alternatively, if the wood is a burr you can simply fill the screw holes which are harder to see when there are lots of little knots.

Pin chuck

Bowls up to 200 mm (8 in) in diameter can be mounted on a pin chuck which is available as an optional extra in a range of sizes with most of the combination chucks. It consists of a spigot of steel with a flat surface on which a pin locates. One end is held in the chuck and the other end is inserted in a hole in the top of the blank which must be drilled precisely the right size and at the correct angle. This chuck relies for its grip on the fact that as the blank rotates slightly the pin tightens against the inside of the hole.

Between the centres (**fig. 35a, page 40**)

I have mentioned this method in the chapter on chucking and the great advantages that it offers are that the wood is safely supported at both ends and you can adjust the angle of the wood while mounting it to get the best from it. The wood is lined up between the centres and can be moved around so that the top is at the angle that you prefer. One of the charms of these bowls is that they give you the opportunity of making asymmetrical objects if you are bored with making everything round. The problem, however, with having a top edge that is lop sided is that when you decide on the shape of the outside a curve that looks right with one part of the top may not look right with another.

Once you have decided on the position of the centres you can remove the blank and prepare the top for the driving centre. It is not a good idea to simply move up the tailstock and force the blank onto the driving centre because the size of the blank will mean that the forks will rotate in the top rather than drive it, particularly if the top is covered with bark which is soft. You must first make sure that you make a good mark where the centre is to

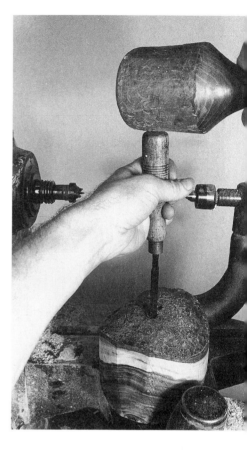

Fig. 110
Marking grooves for driving centre with chisel

Fig. 111
Burr lime with fork centre in hollowed top

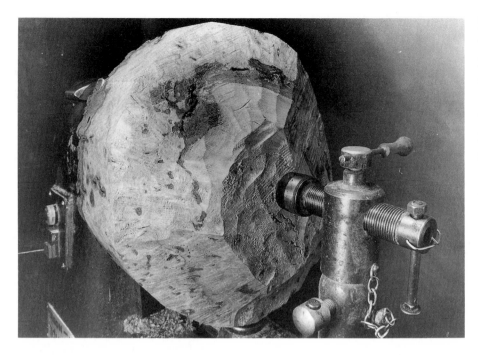

Fig. 112
Burr lime blank showing eccentricities
removed

Fig. 113
Turning outside of lime bowl

be by driving a bradawl well into the wood; then the bark can be removed with a carving gouge or chisel.

When you have established a firm, flat surface you can make indentations in the end to accept the fork centre either by holding a spare one on the centre mark and striking it with a mallet (which will provide enough purchase for a small bowl) or you can make two deeper grooves in the top for the forks to fit in with a chisel (**fig. 110**). In **fig. 111** you can see the driving centre engaged in a hollow in the top of the burr lime blank.

The burr lime blank was asymmetrical to such an extent that it wobbled too much when the lathe started up so I trimmed off some of the eccentricities by hand before starting to turn (**fig. 112**). From this point, shaping the outside can be done with the usual gouges and (just as with the salad bowl) the sides are best shaped from the base (**fig. 113**), although here there is the added reason that you are pushing the blank on to the driving centre.

Your first task is to make the blank round and then you can decide on the shape. The shape of the bottom will be dictated by the type of chuck you have available to hold the bowl for hollowing. For bowls of 150 mm (6 in) and less, such as the laburnum bowl in **fig. 114**, I turn a spigot on the end which can be gripped by either a spigot collet such as that available for use with combination chucks or a dedicated collet chuck as in the case of the laburnum bowl. In these cases the spigot can be incorporated in the design of the bowl if that

Fig. 114
Laburnum blank showing spigot

takes your fancy. You can also hold
a spigot in the external jaws of a
four-jaw chuck but the spigot will
need to be removed or altered after
the bowl is hollowed because it will
show the marks of the jaws.

In the case of bowls larger than
150 mm (6 in), such as the burr
lime, I turn a recess in the base and
hold them in the dovetail jaws of
either a combination chuck or the
Axminster four-jaw or Carlton
chucks. The only problem with this
is that the centre in the base restricts
access but this can be overcome by
making the recess with a cranked
square ended scraper (**fig. 115a–b
and fig. 7, page 15**). **Fig. 116**
shows the recess being marked with
dividers, **fig. 117** shows it being

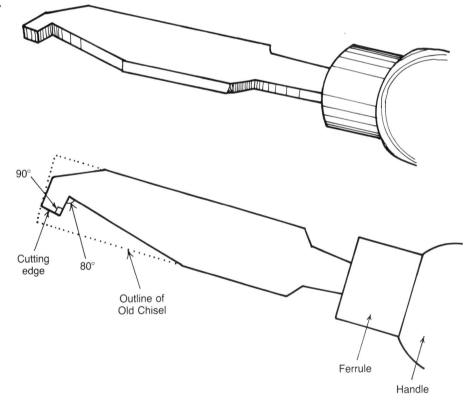

90°

Cutting
edge

80°

Outline of
Old Chisel

Ferrule

Handle

Fig. 115a–b
Cranked square ended scraper

Fig. 116
Marking recess for expanding collets with dividers

Fig. 117
Hollowing recess with 6.25 mm ($\frac{1}{4}$ in) gouge

Fig. 118
Cutting dovetail with cranked scraper

Fig. 119
Cutting spigot with 6.25 mm ($\frac{1}{4}$ in) gouge to break it off

hollowed with a 6.25 mm ($\frac{1}{4}$ in)
gouge and **fig. 118** shows the
cranked scraper in use. The spigot
where the centre engages can be left
so that the bowl can be remounted
between centres, after hollowing,
for finishing off the bottom or it can
be removed at this stage as I did
with the burr Lime (**fig. 119**).

Finishing off the outside

If I am going to turn the still wet
bowl thinly, I like to sand the
outside before hollowing because it
may distort when the inside is taken
out which makes it difficult to sand.
I also like to put some oil on the
outside at this stage because this
delays water escaping from the
outside and therefore slows down
the rate of distortion.

HOLLOWING

This is done with the same tools and
in the same way as in the salad
bowl, the only difference being that,
since the top is not flat, it is not so
easy to judge the correct angle at
which to hold the gouge to start the
cut. You can use a scraper to
establish the rim and provide a stop
for the gouge, but this is more risky
with an uneven top than with a flat
top and this sort of bowl should not
really be tackled until sufficient skill
has been learned to make this
unnecessary. The secret of turning
objects when they are not round is
to treat them as though the outside
of the blurred shape you see is the
surface you are turning, which of
course it is. You can get some idea of
the unevenness of the top from **figs.**

Fig. 120
Hollowing with 12.5 mm ($\frac{1}{2}$ in) gouge, early
in process

Fig. 121
Hollowing with gouge deeper inside

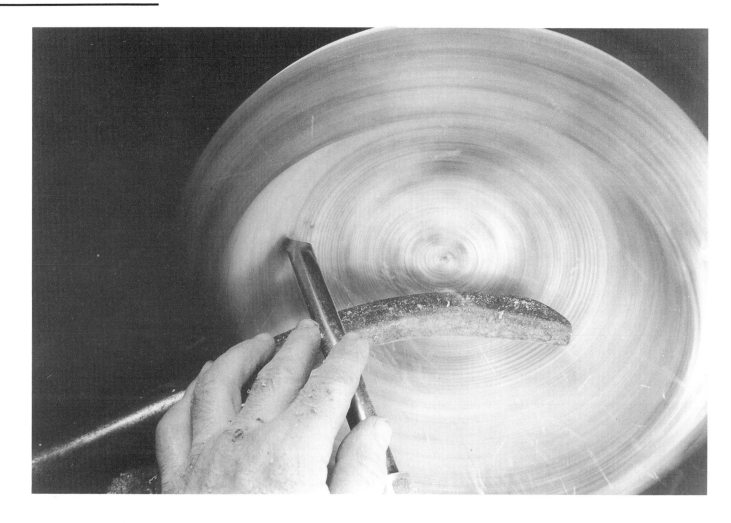

120–121 where the top looks domed before hollowing has made much impression. Because this blank was quite deep I used the home made curved rest (**fig. 85, page 66, and fig. 122**) which enabled me to get the support close to the surface I was turning with the ground back gouge.

When moving or changing rests in the case of natural topped bowls, the lathe must be stopped, as the uneven edges present a real threat to the maintenance of natural digit numbers. The other problem of turning bowls without flat tops is that it is hard to measure the depth, which varies according to which point on the rim you are measuring from. You can get a rough idea of how deep the bowl is by holding a ruler against the side of the bowl and measuring from the top of the blurred edge. To be completely accurate you will need to make a widget like the one in **figs. 123–124** which fits over the chuck at the bottom of the bowl and has calibrated side arms parallel to the axis of the lathe in which is fitted a straight edge. This straight edge can slide up and down the side arms but will stay in place where it rests on the top of the bowl, giving a reference point from which to measure the depth of the bowl.

Fig. 122

Hollowing with ground back gouge on homemade curved rest

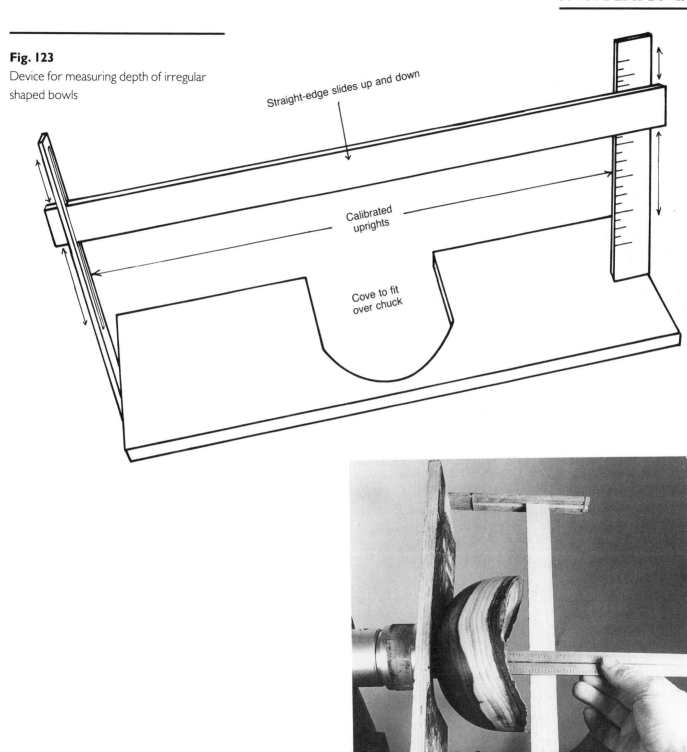

Fig. 123
Device for measuring depth of irregular shaped bowls

Straight-edge slides up and down

Calibrated uprights

Cove to fit over chuck

Fig. 124
Depth measuring device being used in laburnum bowl

Fig. 125
Finishing cut in burr lime bowl

Fig. 126
Sanding inside with 50 mm (2 in) discs

When happy with the depth of the bowl, you can do a smoothing cut with a 6.25 mm ($\frac{1}{4}$in) gouge as in **fig. 125**. Because the grain of burrs is so contrary it is not a good idea to use a scraper inside the bowl. This piece of burr lime was rather soft and the grain tended to tear even with a very sharp gouge. Having soaked the rough parts in cooking oil to make them cut better, I used a power sander to smooth the inside (**figs. 126–127**). See Chapter 5, page 70, for details of the sort of discs used.

If you want to turn a bowl thinly, you must make sure that as you hollow you finish the inside of the walls as they deepen. It is no good thinking that you can do a finishing cut after you have taken out all of the inside because the thin walls will bend away from the tool if there is no thickness in the bottom to steady them. With a flat topped thin bowl you can hold your hand at the rest in such a way that your fingers can rest against the outside of the bowl at the top to hold it against the tool, but this is not possible with an uneven topped bowl if you value your fingers. When you have hollowed below the uneven edge you can use your fingers to steady the outside but great care is needed and this only works where the amount of unevenness does not exceed the capacity of your finger and thumb (**fig. 128**), otherwise you must turn one-handed.

It is even more important to get a good finish from the tool with thin bowls because if you have to do much sanding the uneven thickness of the walls that will result will be very noticeable.

Fig. 127
Sanding further inside

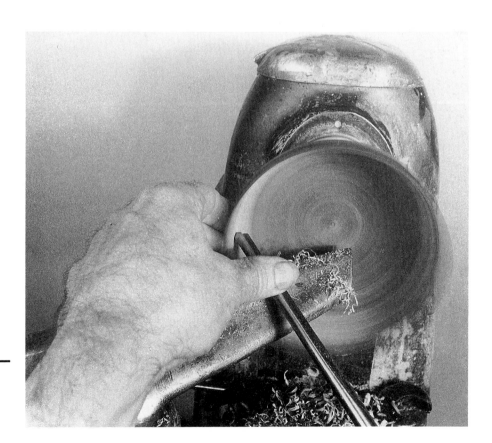

Fig. 128
Finishing cut in laburnum bowl supported
by hand outside

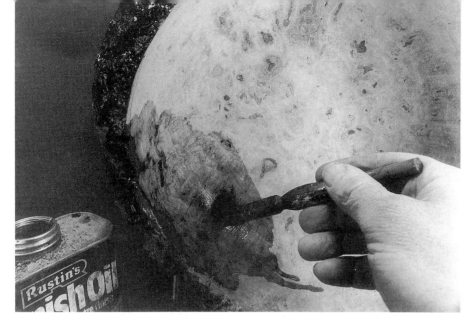

Fig. 129
Applying Danish oil to lime bowl

Fig. 130
Close up of finish

Fig. 131
Distant view of finish

You can finish natural top bowls with vegetable oil and wax as salad bowls or you can use Danish oil or Tung oil because they will probably not be used for food. **Fig. 129** shows Danish oil being applied with a brush and **figs. 130 and 131** show the finish obtained.

REMOUNTING

You cannot use an Axminster chuck with wood jaws for this because of the unevenness of the edge, and with a thin bowl it is not possible to use a specially turned blank to push fit the bowl on because the thin walls will not be strong enough to take the pressure. You can do this with a thick, natural edge bowl, provided the inside shape is not too shallow a curve, but this is where the between-the-centres technique really comes into its own because of the extra support afforded by the tailstock. As I have already mentioned in Chapter 4, page 45, the hollow end needs the support of either a blank of waste wood shaped to fit the inside of the bowl (see **fig. 36b, page 40, and fig. 132**) or the system of foam discs supplied by Craft Supplies (**fig. 36a, page 40, and fig. 133**) where you can see the discs held on by a 25 mm (1 in) pin in a four-jaw chuck.

You can select a combination of discs to fit the inside contours of the bowl (**fig. 134**) and push the bowl onto these with the support of the tailstock (**fig. 135**). The discs do not have to be exactly the same size as the inside of the bowl because they are compressible, but if the walls of

Fig. 132
Burr lime bowl supported on wood blank

Fig. 133
Foam discs on plywood disc and pin in four jaw chuck

Fig. 134
Laburnum bowl being put on foam discs

Fig. 135
Laburnum bowl on foam discs showing spigot

Fig. 136
Laburnum bowl, turning off spigot

the bowl are very thin you may find that they flex rather than the discs, so be careful not to split the bowl when tightening up the tailstock. One problem I have had with these discs is that if the top is asymmetrical the discs will bulge out of the lowest side and not support the bowl centrally, but, apart from this, they are a quick and relatively cheap way of supporting bowls for reverse chucking.

Fig. 136 shows the spigot being turned off. If you want to alter the outside shape at this stage be warned that if the bowl has warped it will be very difficult to blend the shape of the bottom half of the bowl into the top half which is why the shape of the bowl in **fig. 137** (the right hand bowl in **fig. 18**, page 26) has a flat section which makes it a non-saleable item. I made the mistake of leaving this one

overnight before re-turning it.

If you support the bowl on a wooden blank you will need to fit the blank to the lathe and turn it to size which requires repeated checking.

If you make a mistake and it gets too small, all is not lost because you can cover the blank with material to pad it out. This is useful to do anyway to protect the inside of the bowl.

Fig. 137
Laburnum bowl with unsatisfactory shape

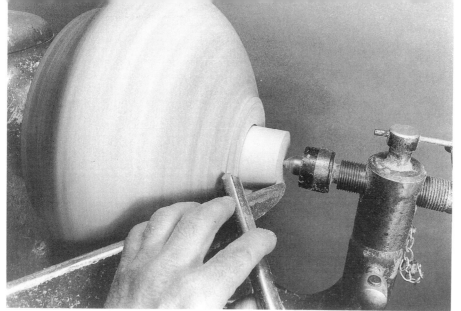

Fig. 138
Turning base of lime bowl with ground back gouge

Fig. 139
Glued on support turned to a small spigot

Fig. 140
Base of lime bowl showing trace of spigot

Fig. 141
Finished base of lime bowl

Even if you did not mount the bowl between centres to start with, you can do so for cleaning up the bottom by gluing a disc of wood to the base for the tailstock to engage in (**figs. 132 and 138**, where the base is being turned with a 12.5 mm ($\frac{1}{2}$ in) gouge).

When I had turned off the base to remove the recess for the expanding chuck, I turned the plug to a small spigot so that I could sand most of the base (**fig. 139**).

When I eventually removed this spigot it left the small mark on the base (**fig. 140**), but I found that the bowl was such a good jam fit on the supporting blank that I could finish the whole bottom on the lathe (**fig. 141**).

If you use the pip left when doing the outside of the bowl between centres, rather than inserting a plug as in the burr lime bowl, you can sand most of the base and remove the pip with a chisel or gouge after removing it from the lathe. If it is a small pip you should be able to sand it so that it cannot be seen.

7
BOWL NESTING DEVICES

When you turn a bowl more wood ends up on the floor than remains in the finished item, and I often regret this waste of solid timber that I have paid for and the tree spent long years producing. The shavings are not wasted for they make good animal bedding and an excellent mulch in the garden, but it would be better if the timber could be used to make bowls. It is clear that this is a common regret among turners for there is a tradition of making nests of bowls from one piece of timber in Austria and Brittany and there is a description of the process in H.V. Morton's book *In Search of England* as carried out on a pole lathe by George Lailey of Buckleberry Common.

Lailey used hook tools which are now in the Museum of English Rural Life in Reading and there are sketches of them in J. Geraint Jenkins' *Traditional Country Craftsmen* (Routledge and Keegan Paul 1966). To be able to do this on a pole lathe must have needed great

Fig. 142
Craft Supplies nesting device removing smallest blank from 300 mm (12 in) × 150 mm (6 in) blank

Fig. 143
Nest of bowls straight from the tool

skill but even with all his skill he used to waste one in six of his attempts.

Increasing concern about the environment and not wasting natural resources have led to modern turners (notably John Ambrose of Cambridgeshire and Cecil Collyer of Dorset) developing their own methods of making nests of bowls that are safer and demand less skill. Craft Supplies have produced a tool on similar principles (see **figs. 142–144**) which will adapt to most lathes.

The principle behind these methods is that of fitting a jig to the lathe which enables a succession of cutters to be used each to cut a successively larger blank from the original blank. The tool invented by Cecil Collyer uses cutters made of strips of high speed steel which are bent to the required diameter and ground so that the faces are also of the same diameter. John Ambrose's tool has a series of different sized cutters brazed onto pivot arms which are approximately quarter hemispheres which he moulds from mild steel and fits to vertical plates.

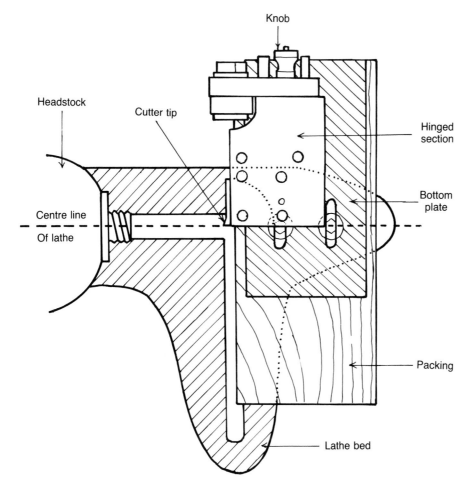

Knob

Headstock

Cutter tip

Hinged section

Bottom plate

Centre line
Of lathe

Packing

Lathe bed

Fig. 144
Craft Supplies nesting device mounted on
Startrite Union Graduate short-bed lathe

CRAFT SUPPLIES BOWL NESTING TOOL

The Craft Supplies model is very similar to John Ambrose's except that the cutters enter the blank from vertically below the centre. This tool can be adapted to different models of lathe by putting packing under the framework to raise its height. The instructions supplied with the tool are basic but I found them

sufficient to get the tool to work. The way to establish the height is by mounting the smallest cutter on the hinged section and then lowering the cutter to the full cutting position so that the tip of the cutter lines up with the centre line of the lathe. In the case of the lathe in the photos, the Startrite Union Graduate bowl turning lathe, the distance between the bed and the centre is 245 mm ($9\frac{7}{8}$ in) which is probably among the largest swings of any mass-produced lathe, and in this case the packing required was 75 mm (3 in).

For the packing I used a piece of ash of the appropriate thickness and I planed it flat because the stability of the device is critical. I found it

necessary to make the packing overhang the bed to the right of the lathe because the rest arm support projects in this way. To counterbalance the projection I made the packing out of a wide enough piece of wood to go over the bed to the left of the lathe, where it benefits from the support of the projection of the bed (see **fig. 144**). The packing that I found to be ideal for my lathe was 450 mm (18 in) × 150 mm (6 in).

The bottom plate of the tool is fitted to the packing with the bolts supplied, provided they are long enough to go through the bottom plate, the packing, the bed and the plate that goes under the bed. In the case of the Graduate they were not so I had to use 200 mm (8 in) bolts.

I then positioned the assembled packing and tool according to instructions, with the smallest cutter mounted, so that it was lined up with the centre of the lathe. I then marked the position of the channel in the bed on the underside of the packing so that I could fit a piece of wood to the underside to run in the channel and prevent the unit from moving from side to side when being used.

The tool is designed to use blanks up to 300 mm (12 in) diameter by 150 mm (6 in) thick and the blank in **figs. 142 and 143** is ash of this size, but I would suggest that it would be prudent for a first attempt with the tool to use a smaller size blank of the softest wood you can lay your hands on.

I shaped the outside of the blank by mounting it on a faceplate and made a recess in the base for the expanding jaws of the Axminster chuck. I then remounted the blank on the chunk and assembled the nesting device on the lathe with the bottom plate parallel to the top face of the blank. You need to know exactly where the centre of the blank is and this is done by holding a pencil at the centre when the blank is rotating. The underside of the cutter plate must be level with the centre dot.

The lathe should run at the slowest available speed and the cutters should be used in sequence of smallest first and largest last if you want the whole range of blanks. The cutter is moved into the blank by using the lever in one hand and holding the other hand on the back of the hinged part. The cutter should be slowly pushed into the wood and frequently removed so that chippings (which can cause the cutter to bind and overheat) can be swept away.

The cutter must be kept very sharp and the best way of doing this is to use a triangular section slipstone.

There is a spring mounted knob (see **fig. 144**) on the upright side of the tool support which is there to hold the cutter backing plate horizontal so that the cutter does not accidentally engage in the blank. I found that if you left this screw adjusted such that it was able to support the cutter in this way while cutting, it prevented the cutter from being removed from the blank to get rid of the chippings. Therefore, it is best to adjust this screw so that it does not project through the upright part while you are cutting.

Eventually the cutter will get

through to the centre of the blank and the little blank can be removed (**fig. 142**) but it is best to be ready for this moment and to stop the lathe immediately to prevent the blank from being snagged on the cutter. The process can then be repeated for each subsequent size of cutter.

If you wish to use the device for blanks of less than 150 mm (6 in) deep the distance of the device from the blank must be adjusted accordingly such that for a 100 mm (4 in) deep blank the device should be 50 mm (2 in) away from the surface.

This device can be used for natural edge bowls but these are more difficult than flat top bowls. You need to be able to remount the blanks to finish them but this is easy using either wooden chucks of the size and shape of the insides or Craft Supplies' foam rubber discs (**fig. 36a**, page 40, and **fig. 133**).

The above devices certainly provide interesting ways of making nests of bowls which result in a saving of valuable timber and, if you are sensible (i.e. you wear a face shield), safe to use. However, they only save you money on timber at the cost of your time. The cutter takes longer to take out the blank than a proficient turner takes to hollow the bowl with a gouge and in the case of the Craft Supplies model, which is the only one you can buy, the cutters take a long time to change because they are held in place with four Allen screws.

If we assume that timber costs £25 per cubic foot a 12 in × 6 in blank will cost £12.50. If you use a nesting device efficiently you

should get from such a blank the following bowls (in inches): 12 × 6, 10 × 5, 8 × 4, 6 × 3 and 4 × 2. At £25 per cubic foot these would cost £12.50, £7.35, £3.73, £1.56, 46 p, a total of £25.60. In other words you have doubled the value of the timber so that if you do not count your time and you have a use for all these sizes of bowls you will recoup the cost of the The Craft Supplies nesting device at £233.39 after you have used up 18 12 × 6 blanks (£233.39 divided by £13.10 = approx 18). That is quite a lot of bowls to the turner who is not full-time but you will save a lot of trees!

For the professional turner the equation is completely altered by the time factor because the saving in timber is much less than the value of the time taken. The most efficient way to use the tool is to prepare a number of blanks and take out the same size blank from each of them in turn before changing the cutter to the next size and going through the process again. Even so the wood would have to be very expensive to make the process commercially viable and I suspect that it would only be really worth taking out the largest size. It is a shame that the largest size available is only 250 mm (10 in) diameter because the biggest savings would be made on blanks of the very largest size. Indeed you can only use the device on blanks of 300 mm (12 in) diameter because the hinge which projects to the side of the bowl as you can see in **fig. 143** (page 97) prevents larger blanks being mounted.

The shape of the blank removed is dictated by the shape of the cutter (see **fig. 145**) and this is inherent in

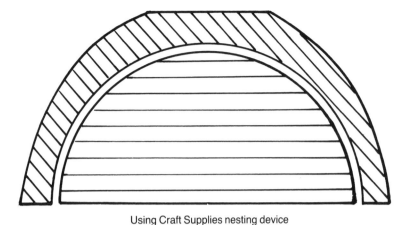

Using Craft Supplies nesting device

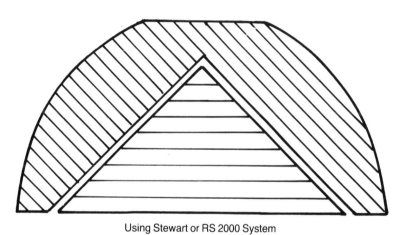

Using Stewart or RS 2000 System

Fig. 145
Relative sizes and shapes of blanks obtainable from within bowls using nesting tool and Stewart or RS 2000 Systems

the basic concept of this type of device. I like this shape of bowl so this aspect does not worry me, and in any case the thickness of the blanks gives scope for altering the shape to some extent. Also, if you just take one 250 mm (10 in) blank from a 300 mm (12 in) blank you can make any shape you like from it.

Once you are proficient in the use of the nesting device you can use any species of wood that you would use for making bowls. You can use unseasoned wood and either leave it to dry or turn the blanks thin and allow then to warp and you can use a natural edged blank. The only problem about the natural edged nest of bowls is that you have to be extra careful when getting to the point when the bowl is about to be separated because, when the bowl breaks free, the highest point on the edge can easily catch on the device as it comes out of the blank and can be damaged.

STEWART OR RS 2000 SYSTEM

Another method of using the wood from the inside of a blank is by separating it with a Stewart System Slicer or a Sorby's RS 2000. The feature common to both systems is a main handle in which can be fitted a variety of tools, one of which is a slicer which can be used to remove the wood from the inside of a bowl in the form of a cone of solid timber. This can be done by turning the outside shape first and then mounting it on a chuck and taking out the cone from the face in the normal hollowing position.

Another way of doing it is to mount the bowl in the normal way (on a faceplate or single screw chuck) and then shape the outside as usual, using the tool to remove the outside bowl from the cone so that the cone remains attached to the faceplate. This will only work if you can get your rest around the bowl between the lathe and the bowl top but the blank may well be more securely attached to the faceplate than it will be when it is reversed onto a chuck where you may want to keep the depth of the recess in the bottom down to a minimum for design considerations. Another well-supported method is to turn the outside shape between centres and use the slicer at this stage.

Although these tools are not bolted to the lathe as the other devices are, they are not difficult to use because the handle of the tool is made to resist the rotational force (an elbow brace in the case of the Stewart system and an adjustable side handle in the case of the RS2000). You can only cut in a straight line with the tool so you have to work out what diameter of blank you want to remove and then guess the angle at which you need to cut so that the point of the cone you will remove meets at the correct depth. You can adjust this angle as you go in but it is best to do it fairly accurately from the start as the tool cuts better if the whole cutting edge cuts at once as opposed to just one side, which is what will happen if you alter the direction of cut.

`Just as in the other devices the tool needs to be removed frequently to remove chippings and the lathe speed should be as slow as possible.

If the cone has not come to a point when the cut is as deep as you can go it may be possible to stop the lathe and break out the blank using a lever of some sort. Beware of doing this when there is more than 37.5 mm ($1\frac{1}{2}$ in) to break through because the grain may tear through the side or bottom of the bowl.

These tools are more flexible than the other devices in so far as you do not use one specific cutter for one size of blank, so you can take out whatever size of blank from the centre as you like. This means that you are not limited to 250 mm (10 in) as the maximum diameter of removed blank and the graduations of the smaller sizes are governed

only by your skill. However, the only shape you can remove is a cone so if you used this device to remove a blank from inside a 300 mm (12 in) diameter blank the resultant piece of wood would be smaller in volume than if you use the nesting device (see **fig. 145**). If you prefer cone shaped bowls this is no problem and if you start with a blank bigger than this you can save more wood with the RS2000 or Stewart tool. It takes a lot less time to set up these tools than the Craft Supplies device and they can also be fitted with a range of different cutters for other uses such as for turning hollow vessels with restricted openings.

AFTERWORD

The previous chapters may well give you enough food for thought to occupy a life time, but there are other directions you may choose to go once you have mastered the basic techniques. You will probably want to do your own exploring but you may like use other turners' work as a starting point – to get ideas I suggest you visit exhibitions and read the woodworking press.

Some people like to decorate basic bowls in plain wood by applying colour or by using them as a vehicle for surface embellishment, by way of hand carving or texturing using an angle grinder or even chainsaw. Others like to cut away large chunks of their bowls such as the bowl shown in Chapter 5, an idea which I have plans to develop.

Adding bits of other media such as metal and glass is not my scene but there are some to whom this appeals. I am more intrigued by hollow forms which in extreme cases require specialized tools and lathes.

Fig. 146
Side view of large platter with lathe rest support

Fig. 147
Front view of large platter

Fig. 148
Turning back of large platter

Making extra large pieces can be fun if you can get large enough planks of wood and in **figs. 142–144** I show that this can be done on a standard lathe simply by removing the rest support and using a second lathe bed as a free standing rest support to give unlimited swing. Such improvisation provides another stepping off point for the explorer in the realms of bowl turning who will never discover all there is to know about this fascinating field.

USEFUL ADDRESSES

EQUIPMENT SUPPLIERS

Lathes

Axminster Power Tool Centre
Chard Street
Axminster
Devon EX13 5DZ
England

LRE Machinery & Equipment Co
Bramco House
Turton Street
Golborne
Warrington WA3 3AB
England

Craft Supplies Ltd
The Mill
Miller's Dale
Buxton
Derbyshire SK17 8SN
England

Craft Supplies USA
1287 East 1120 South
Provo
UT 84606
USA

Tools

Robert Sorby Ltd
Athol Road
Sheffield S80 0PA
England

Henry Taylor (Tools) Ltd
The Forge
Lowther Road
Sheffield S6 2DR
England

Jerry Glaser Co., Inc
P.O. Box 2417
Newport Beach
CA 92663
USA

Multistar Machine and Tool Ltd
Ashton House
Wheatfield Road
Colchester CO3 5YA
England

Airstream dust helmets

Equipment suppliers as above plus

Airstream Dust Helmets
P.O. Box 975
Elbow Lake
MN 56561
USA

RECOMMENDED READING

Art Forms in Nature, Karl Blossfeldt, Zwemmer, 1967

Form in Nature and in Life, Andreas Feininger, Thames and Hudson, 1966

Theory of Design, Peter C. Gasson, B.T. Batsford Ltd, 1974

A Potter's Book, Bernard Leach, Faber and Faber, 3rd edition 1976

The Nature and Art of Workmanship, David Pye, Cambridge University Press, 1988

The Evolution of Designs, Biological analogy in architecture and the applied arts, Philip Steadman, Cambridge University Press, 1979

Turned Bowl Design, Richard Raffan, The Taunton Press, Inc., 1987

Ceramic Form, Peter Lane, Collins, 1988

Artistic Woodturning, Dale Nish

The Woodworker's Pocket Book, Charles Hayward, Harper Collins, 1992

INDEX